French General

A YEAR OF
JEWELRY

To Sofia...
Who grew up in a house filled
with beads, buttons, and baubles
and never complained.

An Imprint of Sterling Publishing
387 Park Avenue South
New York, NY 10016

© 2015 by Kaari Meng
Photography © 2015 by Jon Zabala
Design by French General

ISBN 978-1-4547-0804-9

Distributed in Canada by Sterling Publishing
c/o Canadian Manda Group, 165 Dufferin Street
Toronto, Ontario, Canada M6K 3H6
Distributed in the United Kingdom by GMC Distribution Services
Castle Place, 166 High Street, Lewes, East Sussex, England BN7 1XU
Distributed in Australia by Capricorn Link (Australia) Pty. Ltd.
P.O. Box 704, Windsor, NSW 2756, Australia

For information about custom editions, special sales, and premium and corporate purchases,
please contact Sterling Special Sales at 800-805-5489 or specialsales@sterlingpublishing.com.

Manufactured in China

2 4 6 8 10 9 7 5 3 1

larkcrafts.com

French General

A YEAR OF
JEWELRY

36 PROJECTS WITH VINTAGE BEADS

KAARI MENG

LARK

CONTENTS

A WORD TO CREATIVE TYPES...

This jewelry book is inspired by the seasonal changes in France. All of the chapters use inspiration based on French holidays and events throughout the French calendar. I tend to design jewelry with the vintage beads I have found over the years—so it is doubtful that you will be able to find the exact same beads to design your own projects. I encourage you to look in your own stash of beads, or visit a flea market or thrift shop and repurpose an old piece of jewelry— cut out the best beads and combine them with other bits and pieces you may have been saving for a rainy day. Use this book as a guide to help you find your color palette and jewelry style…if a certain technique is driving you crazy, move on and try another. The important thing is to spend a little time every day making jewelry so your craft improves over time. Most of all, have fun and make something new to share with someone!

Merci—

Kaari

BASICS

OVER THE YEARS, I HAVE LEARNED THAT MAKING GOOD JEWELRY IS MADE UP OF THREE BASICS... GOOD MATERIALS, GOOD TOOLS, AND GOOD TECHNIQUES. THROUGHOUT THIS CHAPTER, I WILL TALK ABOUT THE MATERIALS I ENJOY DESIGNING JEWELRY WITH, THE TOOLS I LIKE WORKING WITH, AND THE TECHNIQUES I MOST OFTEN USE. THIS IS JUST THE TIP OF THE ICEBERG...THERE ARE HUNDREDS, IF NOT THOUSANDS, OF IDEAS THAT COULD BE COVERED, BUT I WILL STICK TO WHAT I KNOW AND TALK MOSTLY ABOUT THE JEWELRY I HAVE BEEN DESIGNING OVER THE PAST TWENTY-FIVE YEARS.

MATERIALS

I love the entire process of making jewelry, but the hunt for the perfect materials is my favorite part. If you start to see everything as a potential jewelry component, you can begin to create unique jewelry with bits from the past—old buttons, glass rings, seashells and charms can all be reused.

My favorite objects to collect and use in jewelry making are vintage and old. When I first started collecting glass beads, bits and baubles, almost twenty-five years ago, I thought "the older, the better." I collected almost anything wrapped in old paper or hidden in dark basements. After amassing an enormous stash of antique and vintage beads, I eventually had to change my bead buying and started collecting only what appealed to me most...which is just about anything that is inspired by nature, including Murano hand-pulled glass leaves on wire, old mother-of-pearl buttons, and pressed-glass flowers.

If you're still learning what colors, shapes, and types of components you like, study different pieces of jewelry. Go to museums, craft stores, bead shops, flea markets, and thrift stores, or scour local garage sales on a Saturday morning. Looking at jewelry, old and new, is a great way to help you decide what fits your personal style. I think it's ok to be inspired by others, just be sure to put your unique design into everything you do… design your pieces as an expression of who you are.

VINTAGE BEADS

Beads pop up in the most unusual places. One of my favorite unexpected finds was at an old millinery workshop that made silk flowers. While digging through crates of old feathers and flowers, I found a box full of early bright red glass cherries that were embedded with wire. I quickly used all of them in my designs, but I still think about the find and remember how surprised I was to have unearthed them in a flower making workshop.

Old beads engage many of your senses. The smoothness of blown or molded glass, colors both vivid and muted, matte or shiny finishes, the weight of each bead, the way the hanks are strung together, and the original packaging or labels—all of these physical characteristics will give you clues to the age of the beads and, with any luck, where they were made.

Flea markets, bead shows, and bead shops are the best places to check out beads up close (be sure not to overlook the selection online). Search for the colors and shapes that speak to you. If you're drawn to organic colors and shapes, look for seashell, horn, coral, or wooden beads. If you love the appearance of hand-blown glass or lampwork beads, go to craft or bead shows and seek out artisans who make their own beads. And if your work lends itself to the ethnic, African or early American Indian trade beads are true beauties.

When looking for vintage beads, I always consider the condition first. If a bead is peeling or over oxidized, I usually pass it by. The last thing I want is for a vintage bead to deteriorate once I have used it in a piece of jewelry. If the bead has good patina or looks like is has

held up well for the past twenty, thirty, or even eighty years…then I don't hesitate! The more you look at old beads and materials the easier you will be able to spot the useable pieces.

From the 1920s through the 1970s, Providence, Rhode Island, was the bead capital of the United States, and it's still a great place to start digging around for old glass beads. You can also do an online search for close-out bead dealers—these are the guys that are buying out the bead warehouses when they close up after fifty years of business. If you're willing to travel, many of these close-out warehouses will let you rummage through their old stock and purchase by the pound, but some have caught on that vintage materials have gone up in value and they now sell by the dozen or even the piece. One thing to keep in mind: buying vintage beads and materials can add up fast…a box full of old glass beads could end up costing you more than a box of new beads!

Meeting vendors at a bead show is another great way to find interesting suppliers of old materials. Over the years, I have developed some wonderful relationships with bead dealers who may not have exactly what I am looking for at the time, but keep me in mind when they uncover something interesting. Every once in a while, I will get a call from a vendor who has just come across a basement full of old French steel cut beads or glass and mother of pearl buttons still on their original cards.

Old glass is a great collectible and it will go up in value. Once you know what's right for you, buy as much of it as you can afford. I try to buy the whole box of beads or buttons whenever possible. If I can't afford the whole lot, I'll ask the dealer to hold onto the supply until I have the money for the rest. Sometimes, offering to take the whole box or lot will allow you to negotiate a better price.

REPRODUCTION BEADS

In the Czech Republic, glassmaking is an age-old cottage industry, and that's where the majority of reproduction beads are made today. Generally made by hand with original molds and colors, these beautiful beads have the look and feel of the originals, but at a far more reasonable price. You'll find shapes and colors that haven't been seen in more than fifty years—basic forms such as donut, square, round, cathedral, dagger, teardrop, and rondelles, as well as novelties like fruits, animals, hearts, and leaves. You'll locate these reproduction beads easily in bead stores and online, sold by the strand or by the gross (144 pieces).

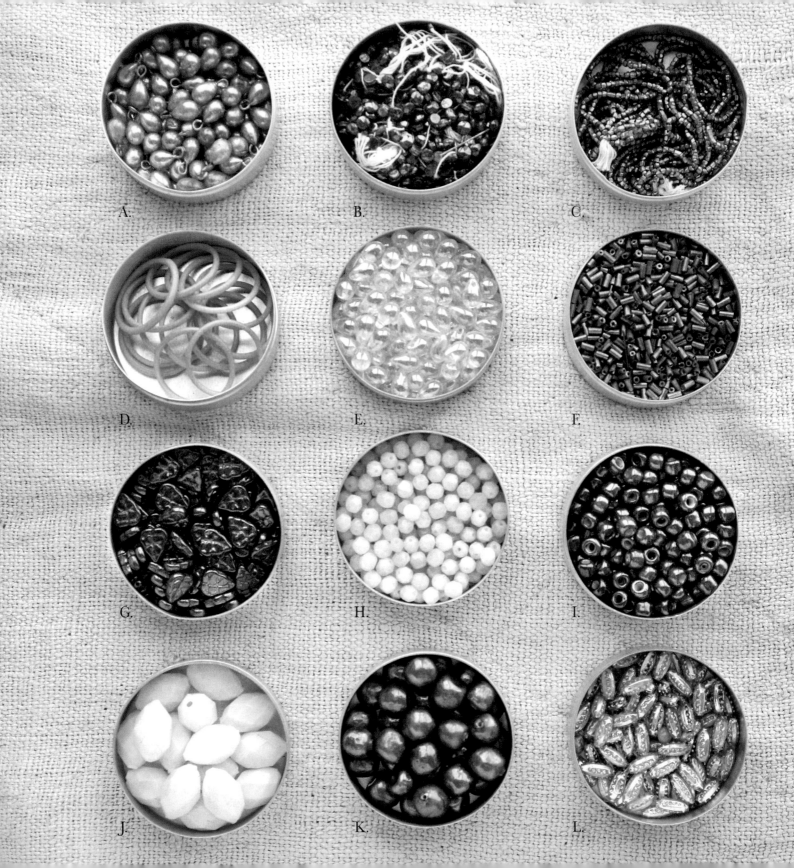

A.

B.

C.

D.

E.

F.

G.

H.

I.

J.

K.

L.

SOME TYPES OF VINTAGE GLASS BEADS

A. Embedded wire beads have a wire permanently sunk into the glass. This makes it easy to loop these beads onto a chain or to use them as pendants.

B. Nailhead beads are flat on the back, with a front that looks like a hammered rivet or the head of a nail. Many were produced between 1920 and 1930 for the French garment industry.

C. Seed beads are tiny, round beads, most of them about ¾ in. (2 mm) or smaller. Each size is given a number, such as 11° (which is pronounced 11 ott). The larger the number, the smaller the bead.

D. Glass rings are thin, fused glass rods that come in circular, oval, or square shapes. Made in Japan, they're extremely lightweight and fragile.

E. Side-drilled beads, as opposed to center-drilled beads, are beads that are drilled side-to-side and usually look great when strung together.

F. Bugle beads are small, tubular-shaped beads that vary in length from ⅛ in. (3 mm) to 2 ½ in. (6.4 cm). Like seed beads, they're usually used in very small work and seen in bead-weaving designs.

G. Pressed-glass beads are made exactly as they sound—by pressing glass into a mold—and they're some of the highest-quality beads out there. Many shapes can be made this way, with intricate patterns imprinted onto the bead.

H. Opal glass beads, or sea opal glass beads, imitate opal stones by using a bluish luminescent glass base.

I. Pony or trading beads were first introduced to American Indians by French explorers in the early seventeenth century and were immediately popular and well suited for use in decorating their garments. Pony beads usually have a nice large hole ideal for leather stringing.

J. Hollow glass beads, popular throughout the nineteenth and twentieth centuries offer a lightweight bead, that is extremely delicate but wonderful for making clustered jewelry.

K. Glass pearls are round glass beads with a pearlized coating. Sometimes manufactured with a lead base, these pearls can have a nice heft and are a great imitation of real pearls.

L. Mercury glass, also known as silvered glass, contains neither mercury nor silver. Made in France and Japan, these beads are hollow glass, coated on the inside with a silvering formula.

VIALLA

hommes et enfants

Toques, Grecques et

Fantaisie de Paris

Articles sur mesure

Anglaise, etc. Palmiers

fins et communs

Nouveautés de la Saison

Ville et Campagne

Rue de la Fontaine et rue de la Boucherie

A VILLEFRANCHE (AVEYRON)

CABOCHONS

Cabochons are flat backed stones or glass pieces that are typically set or glued into a bezel to make a charm, pendant, or earring. Cushion back cabochons have a faceted or cushion-cut back that requires them to be set into a cup or prong-setting bezel.

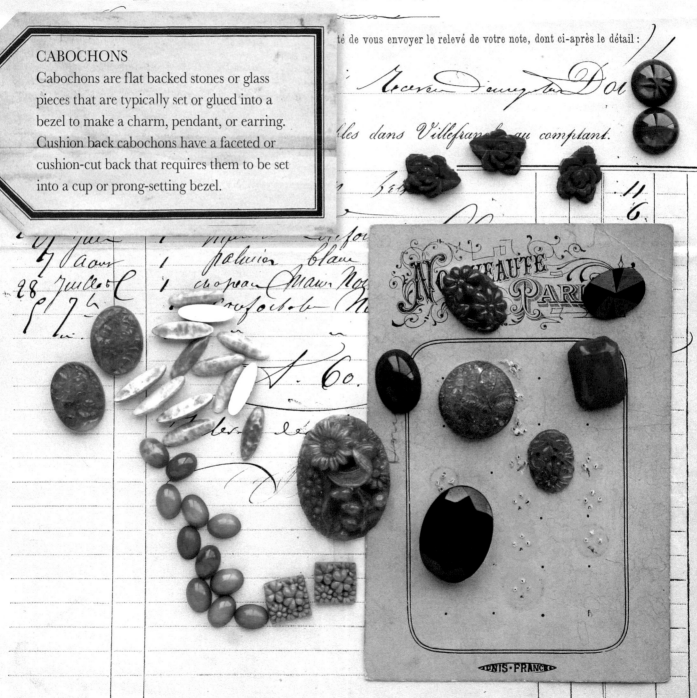

CHARMS

If you can drill a hole in it and hang a jump ring on it, it's a charm! Old religious medals, stamped brass pieces of metal, cast metal trinkets, bone rings, and metal hardware are all interesting elements that can become a part of jewelry design. Old game pieces such as bingo chips or dice make a great charm   simply drill a small hole in the top of a die and screw an eyelet into it, and you have an instant charm.

Stampings are very thin sheets of brass imprinted with dies to produce cutouts such as charms or filigree. In the 1930s and '40s, these pretty bits of metal lace, called filigree, were a staple of costume jewelry; and they're currently enjoying a well-deserved resurgence in popularity. Back in the day, filigree stampings were beaded using a thin-gauge plated wire to sew small beads onto the brass stamping; this is referred to as cagework.

A.

B.

C.

D.

E.

F.

JEWELRY FINDINGS

Findings are the component parts or materials that hold a piece of jewelry together, and there are all sorts of them available, most are metal and available in a number of finishes or metal colors, to complement your jewelry. Some of my favorite plating or finishes include honey brass-ox, antique silver, gunmetal, and black-ox. Many people choose to stick with one metal finish or color when designing a piece of jewelry, but mixing up metal colors can achieve beautiful results— and it's a whole lot easier when using vintage materials because you don't have to find the perfect color match. Some of the findings I use regularly are: head pins, eye pins, clasps, crimp beads, ear wires, jump rings, bezels, and stampings.

A. HEAD PINS are short pieces of wire with a flat head on one end, like a nail, that prevents a strung-on bead from falling off. They come in ½-in. to 2 ½-in. (1.3 cm to 6.35 cm) lengths and can vary in gage from soft to hard. I typically use a 1-in. (2.5 cm) head pin in a medium, or 26, gage. Head pins are used for making bead dangles and attaching beads to loops in jewelry. Ball-end head pins add a decorative touch to any design.

B. EYE PINS are short lengths of wire with a pre-made loop at one end, available in lengths from ½-in. to 3 in. (1.3 cm to 7.6 cm). I like the 1in. (2.5 cm) length best, again in a 26 gage. Eye pins are used to link beads together—especially when making a rosary-chain style necklace or bracelet—which is simply a bead link-to-link length of chain.

C. CRIMP BEADS are tiny metal beads used to secure both ends of a necklace or bracelet strung with nylon cord. They also work well when stringing beads on elastic to hold the first bead in place, or to cover the knot.

D. CLASPS connect the ends of a necklace or bracelet. Lobster clasps, spring rings, toggles, and swivel clasps are some of my favorites. I like using clasps in the front of a necklace to hold a collection of old charms.

E. EAR WIRES are the components that help you make up a pair of earrings. A few different types exist, including the French wire, as well as a lever-back style that prevents earrings from falling out.

F. JUMP RINGS are small metal rings made out of wire (typically $1/64$ in. [3 mm], $13/64$ in. [5 mm], and $5/16$ in. [3 mm], in diameter) with a split in them so that you can open and close them. You'll use them to connect chains, charms, and clasps, among other things, to your jewelry.

Bezels are metal frames or disks for showcasing cabochons. Many bead stores that carry cabochons will carry bezels to match. You'll find both flat-back bezels, onto which you can glue a cab, and prong bezels that have a deeper cup to accommodate cushion-back cabochons or bezels. When you buy them, they'll probably be shiny, but they tend to oxidize nicely over time. To accelerate the process, rub a mix of black and brown acrylic paint onto raw brass pieces, wipe it off after 30 seconds, and then seal it with a lacquer to hold the color.

CHAIN

There are many different types of chain, and each one allows you to design a different silhouette for a necklace or bracelet. There are cable chains, curb chains, figaro chains, rope chains, dap bar chains…the list goes on and on. I enjoy using found materials to make my own chain styles, including old rosary chains, buttons glued onto flat round disks, and rings connected together to make up a length of chain.

Choosing a chain depends on what you are going to add to it and what style necklace or bracelet you want to design. A good rule of thumb is to find a chain link size you enjoy wearing, and chances are you'll enjoy working with it.

My favorite chain to use is the cable or link chain. Cable chains are made up of uniformed sized rings that can be round or oval. When I begin working with a chain, I am always aware of the front, back, top, and bottom—so I am sure to be consistent with hanging charms or beads; this is especially important when designing a necklace and you want the elements to all hang forward.

STRINGING MATERIALS

There are all sorts of way to string a strand of beads—and each material will give you a different effect. A silk string or cord will give a classic look to a necklace, while a leather or hemp cord will give a more ethnic look to your jewelry designs.

NYLON CORD is a nylon-coated wire perfect for basic bead stringing, available in either a three- or seven-strand diameter. Finish nylon cord by using a crimp bead, split ring, and clasp.

LEATHER CORD is typically available in a couple of different widths and finishes. Knot the ends to finish them, or use a crimping clasp, which has the crimp bead set into the clasp.

SILK CORD is wonderfully smooth and soft against the skin, comes in many colors, and creates the nicest drape on a necklace. Silk has been the traditional stringing material for centuries. Silk cord can be finished with a triple knot and a bead cap, the first and last finding you string onto your piece. When you're shopping, ask for the silk cord that comes with a thin, built-in needle that allows you to bead the tiniest of seed beads.

WAX CORD or HEMP are easy to thread and visually, they don't look heavy. Because they resist twisting or knotting, these are a good choice for long necklaces with multiple charms. Finish the ends with crimping beads and a clasp, or knot them.

ELASTIC CORD comes in a variety of colors and widths. This strong material can be finished by triple knotting and securing with a spot of glue, or by using a crimp bead to cover the knot.

RIBBON and other fibers offer a charming way to add texture to jewelry. Close necklaces or bracelets with a length of silk ribbon tied into a dainty bow. Or thread a bracelet with a bit of ribbon to convert it into a necklace. Weave small bits of old fibers through chain, or tie them to jump rings. Ribbons can be finished by crimping a ribbon clasp onto each end, or just adding a stitch or two with needle and thread.

TOOLS

I have always believed that having a good set of jewelry
tools on hand makes jewelry designing much easier! If you
can invest in a better set of tools, you will have them for
a lifetime. I use either the "all in one" plier or a few basic
tools, depending upon my project.

PLIERS

ROUND-NOSE PLIERS, preferably with a side cutter, which I refer to as an "all in one" plier makes wire looping a breeze, because you don't have to set down your pliers constantly to pick up the wire cutters.

FLAT-NOSE PLIERS are for opening and closing jump rings. Many people find it easier on their fingers to open and close jump rings with two flat-nose pliers—once you practice this a bit it becomes quite easy. You can also use flat nose pliers to crumple crimp beads or tubes if you don't have crimping pliers.

CRIMPING PLIERS are designed to crimp, crumple, or crush tubular crimp beads and securely connect beading wires to clasps.

CUTTING PLIERS are for cutting wire, eye pins, and head pins, as well as most stringing materials, including silk cord and elastic.

When working on small pieces, it's good to also have a smaller pair of flat-nose pliers and round-nose pliers for wire wrapping and wire looping. I store all of my tools, including a tube of glue in a hemp roll that ties easily and keeps tools safe and clean. A tool roll allows you to travel easily with your tools at a moment's notice.

ADHESIVES

I've been searching for the perfect glue ever since I began designing jewelry more than twenty-five years ago. Every brand on the market has its own consistency and characteristics. Some are good for glass, others work well with metal, and some are best for more porous materials like mother-of-pearl. The most important thing to remember when you start to work with glue is…patience! The longer you let something set after you have glued it, the better the glue will adhere the two pieces together. Also, it's important to remember that glued charms should not be exposed to heat or moisture—both of these elements will affect the glue and could cause the two pieces to come apart.

STRONG-HOLD GLUE, like Super Glue, is great for quick projects because it sets very quickly. However, it leaves you no time to reset or adjust a piece.

TWO-PART EPOXY works well, but there can be an element of waste because the epoxies have to be mixed together on a glue card, and if you don't use it within a couple of minutes the mixture hardens.

MULTI-USE GLUE, like Beacon's 527, is what I'm using the most these days. It sets fast but still gives you a little time to readjust items, is water proof, and dries crystal clear. I am sensitive to toxic glue scents, and this glue has a very low scent.

OTHER USEFUL ITEMS

A few other items I like to have to have on hand while making jewelry include: a small pair of scissors for cutting cords or elastic, a ruler or tape measure to measure lengths of chain or stringing material, a sliding brass gauge, or caliper, to measure bead or cabochon sizes, and, a beading mat or a soft material to put your beads on so they don't roll around.

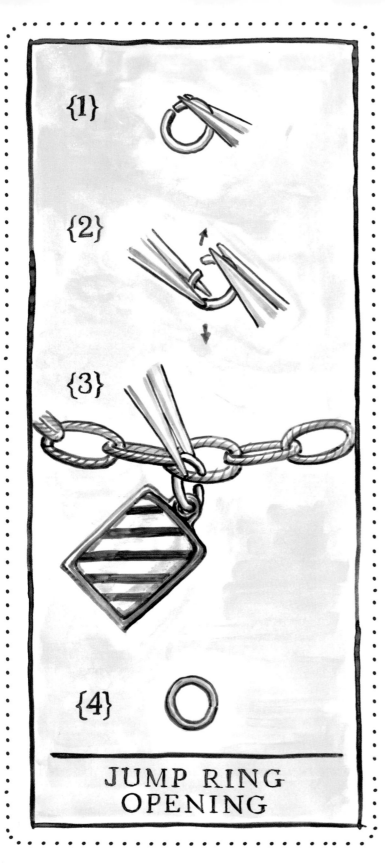

{1}

{2}

{3}

{4}

JUMP RING OPENING

TECHNIQUES

There are all sorts of techniques that can be used when making jewelry, and designers have their own way of making techniques work for them. Looking up any of these techniques online or on YouTube will give you a visual that is very helpful. Here are a few of my tips on how I work with different materials and findings while I am designing jewelry:

OPENING AND CLOSING JUMP RINGS

Learning to open and close a jump ring properly takes a bit of time, but once done correctly, your jump rings should be secure and will not allow elements to drop off your jewelry. While practicing this technique, if you distort the shape of the jump ring, set aside and start over with a new jump ring. A damaged or bent jump ring will not withstand the test of time.

Think of a jump ring like a clock face, and put the split part of the ring at the midnight hour. Using your flat-nose plier, pinch the ring at 3:00, then with your left forefinger and thumb—or another pair of flat-nose pliers—pinch the ring at 9:00. Your pliers should be holding on tight to the ring on each side. Push away from you with your right hand and pull toward you with your left hand—and split the ring open. Don't be afraid to make a nice wide split—it's easier to work with. Once you have attached your charm, clasp, or chain to the ring and are ready to close it, you will do the opposite motion. So, your right hand—still pinching the ring at 3:00—will pull toward you and your left hand—still pinching the ring at 9:00—will push away from you.

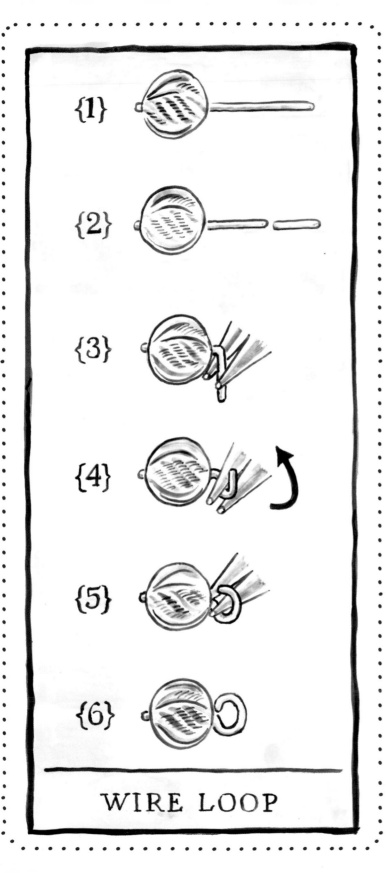

{1}

{2}

{3}

{4}

{5}

{6}

WIRE LOOP

Now here's the secret tip….instead of just trying to match up the wire at the top, go past the midnight hour—so push the left side of the ring past the right side—and then pull it back so it settles into place. The ring should be flush, without a gap and if you are lucky, you will even hear it click closed—then you know it is secure and locked.

WIRE LOOP

To link wire you can use eye pins, head pins, or a roll of 24–28 gage wire. To start with a 1-in. (2.5-cm) head or eye pin, thread the bead through, and cut the wire down to about ½ in. (1.3 cm) above the bead. Using your round-nose pliers, bend wire back to a 90° angle against the bead. Grab the wire with the pliers and roll the wire around the nose of the pliers toward the bead. Leave a bit of a gap if you are going to connect this part to your chain or another eye pin. Once you have connected pin to your chain or eye pin, go back in with your round-nose pliers and close the gap. The important key here is to make sure that the wire is totally closed, because if it is at all open, something will end up falling off your jewelry. Eventually, your loops will look rounder and be more consistent in size. Remember, where you grab the wire to bend it around the pliers determines your loop size, so if you want consistent loops, try grabbing the wire in the same place every time you loop.

USING BEAD CAPS

When beginning to string a piece of jewelry on silk thread or cord, tie a triple knot at the one end and then thread on a bead cap with the opening facing toward the knot. Add a drop of glue onto the knot and the cover the knot with the bead cap. Using your flat-nose pliers, gently close the bead cap and trim off any excess string.

Continue to thread your beads onto the string and then do the same technique on the opposite end of the thread when you are finished beading. Be sure to keep the beads taut so that there is no gap left between the beads after knotting the two ends.

GLUING CHARMS OR CABOCHONS

The secret to gluing is to cover the whole surface of the back of the charm or cabochon with glue. Remember a little glue goes a long way. Be sure to set your glue tube tip up—or rest it in a glass in between using—so the glue doesn't continue to ooze out.

On a flat surface, set the cabochon into place on the bezel. Watch this for a minute or two in case it slides around a bit. Allow the components to set for at least an hour before using. While waiting for charms to dry, you can begin to layout the rest of your design.

GLUING CUSHION-CUT CABOCHONS

If using a cushion-cut cabochon, fill the cup of the bezel with glue, to just below the top of the bezel. Set the cabochon into the setting, place on a flat surface, and allow to set for at least an hour. If your bezel has prong settings, allow the piece to dry completely before using your flat-nose pliers to fold down the prongs. Pressing the prongs into a flat surface—like a worktable—and rolling forward softly can help.

NOW THAT YOU HAVE READ THE BASICS OF JEWELRY MAKING, COLLECT YOUR MATERIALS AND FIND A WELL-LIT, QUIET SPACE TO EXPERIMENT WITH COLOR, TEXTURE, AND DESIGN. REMEMBER TO USE THE FOLLOWING PAGES AS INSPIRATION AND CREATE YOUR OWN JEWELRY WITH MATERIALS YOU HAVE ON HAND. IF A DESIGN CALLS FOR 5 MM WHITE PEARLS AND ALL YOU HAVE ARE 7 MM WHITE GLASS BEADS, BY ALL MEANS, USE THE BEADS YOU HAVE! PART OF THE FUN OF MAKING VINTAGE-INSPIRED JEWELRY IS USING BEADS FROM YOUR COLLECTION... OR COLLECTIONS YOU HAVE FOUND AT FLEA MARKETS, THRIFT STORES, OR ESTATE SALES.

HAVE FUN!

BASICS STEPS TO CREATE A CHARM BRACELET

1. Separate your materials, including headpins, jumprings, clasp, and chain.

2. Match up cabachons to bezels.

3. Glue cabachons to matching bezels.

4. Let cabachons and bezels dry for at least 1 hour.

5. Using flat-nose pliers, open medium jump ring and thread through clasp.

6. Attach clasp at one end of 7½-in. (190.5-mm) cut of chain; close jump ring.

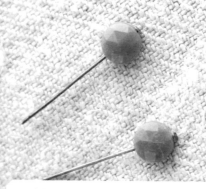

10. Thread headpin through small bead and then through button, the small bead prevents the larger button from falling off of headpin.

11. Using round-nose pliers push wire to a 90° angle.

12. Roll wire around round-nose pliers nose to create a loop.

16. Use small accent beads to fill in spaces. Thread beads with headpins and cut wire to ½ in. (1.3 cm).

17. Using round-nose pliers, push wire to a 90° angle and roll wire around pliers to create a loop.

18. Place each bead on chain and close loop.

7. Once cabachons are dry, attach with flat-nose pliers and small jump ring.

8. Open jump ring, attach to chain.

9. Close jump ring to secure charm will not fall off.

13. Attach loop to chain.

14. Close wire with pliers to secure button on chain.

15. Continue to add other charms and cabachons with jump rings.

19. Continue to add on small beads to chain.

JANVIER

LE JOUR DE L'AN

Bonne Année! French streets and homes ring out with cheery wishes of "Happy New Year"! As friends, family, and strangers don their fanciest dress and gather to celebrate La Saint Sylvestre on December 31, and dance into the wee hours of Le Jour de l'An (New Year's Day). New Year's Eve gatherings are likely to be costume parties or elaborate dinners featuring oysters, foie gras, smoked salmon, and Champagne.

Material Inspiration: ruby pinks, pale dusty pinks, grassy greens, chateau keys and crowns to ring in a regal, festive jewelry set.

REMOVABLE CHARMS

The beauty of removable charms is they allow you the versatility of deciding which charms to wear on any given day. Attach an 8-mm jump ring to each of your charms so they can be added easily or removed, depending on your mood. Attach a larger clasp to your designs so you can easily add on four to six charms. When not using your extra charms, store them in a nearby jewelry box so they'll always be handy.

LE JOUR DE L'AN NECKLACE

Glue each of the glass cabochons to their corresponding brass bezels. Set them aside to dry.

Cut the chain into seven pieces 3 in. (7.6 cm) long and seven pieces 4 in. (10.2 cm) long.

Thread an eye pin through each milky cranberry glass bead and form them into six linked sections containing four beads each, and six linked lengths of three beads each.

Connect the linked beads with pieces of chain to make a long chain measuring 64 in. (1.6 m).

Using a 5-mm jump ring, attach the swivel clasp at one end of the long chain. On the opposite end of the chain, attach the watch clasp with a 5-mm jump ring.

Link together two rose-colored 6-mm rose beads using eye pins, and connect them to the large pink glass charm.

Dangle all the charms and the beaded flower from the swivel clasp using the 8-mm jump rings.

BEADS & CHARMS

52 milky cranberry glass beads, 10 mm
1 pink glass cabochon, 20 x 25 mm
1 pink glass cabochon, 10 x 15 mm
1 brass crown charm, 20 x 40 mm
1 brass key charm, 55 mm
2 rose-colored glass beads, 6 mm
1 beaded flower, 50 mm

FINDINGS

1 brass bezel, 20 x 25 mm
1 brass bezel, 10 x 15 mm
5 brass jump rings, 8 mm
2 brass jump rings, 5 mm
54 brass eye pins, 1 inch (2.5 cm)
1 brass swivel clasp, 20 mm
1 brass watch clasp, 20 mm
48 in. (1.2 m) of small brass cable chain

TOOLS

Round-nose pliers
Flat-nose pliers
Cutting pliers
Jewelry glue

HELPFUL TIPS

LAYERING CHARMS

To make unique charms, consider layering additional bezels and cabochons on top of flat-top cabochons. To do this, glue your base cabochon into a bezel and let it dry completely. Then glue on a smaller bezel and cabochon positioned nicely as a focal point for the finished charm. Make sure you let all glued pieces dry completely before wearing them. Add an 8-mm jump ring to each to make the charm interchangeable.

LE JOUR DE L'AN BRACELET

DIRECTIONS

Glue all the cabochons into their respective bezels and set them aside to dry.

Connect the watch clasp to one end of the chain using a 5-mm jump ring.

Connect the 8-mm jump ring to the other end of the chain.

Thread the 13 glass rose beads with head pins.

Starting from the side with the watch clasp, cut and link three of them onto the first three cable links.

Thread a head pin into a milky cranberry glass bead and connect it on the fourth cable link. Continue with this pattern along the entire length of chain.

Arrange the design of the bracelet in such a way as to balance out all of the beads with the charms and beaded glass drops.

Connect the charms and drops using the 3-mm or 5-mm jump rings.

BEADS & CHARMS

13 rose-colored glass beads, 6 mm
5 rose-colored seed bead flower stamens, 15 mm
4 milky cranberry beads, 10 mm
4 gray oval glass cabochons, 10 x 11 mm
1 pink and gold glass domed cabochon, 14 x 20 mm
1 milky cranberry glass cabochon, 13 mm
1 milky cranberry glass cabochon, 10 x 12 mm
1 mother-of-pearl cabochon, 20 x 25 mm
1 mother-of-pearl cabochon, 20 mm
1 milky gray glass cabochon, 9 mm
1 crystal cross, 5 mm
1 brass cross charm, 16 x 24 mm
1 brass crown charm, 20 x 40 mm
1 brass crest charm, 25 x 35 mm
2 brass crown charms, 15 x 25 mm
4 brass oval bezels, 10 x 11 mm
1 oval brass bezel, 14 x 20 mm
1 round brass bezel, 13 mm
1 oval brass bezel, 20 x 25 mm
1 round brass bezel, 20 mm
1 oval brass bezel, 10 x 12 mm
1 round brass bezel, 9 mm

FINDINGS

13 brass jump rings, 3 mm
8 brass jump rings, 5 mm
1 brass jump ring, 8 mm
17 brass head pins, 1 inch (2.5 cm)
1 brass watch clasp, 12 mm
7½ in. (19 cm) of medium brass cable chain

TOOLS

Round-nose pliers
Flat-nose pliers
Cutting pliers
Jewelry glue

LE JOUR DE L'AN EARRINGS

DIRECTIONS

Using wire cutters, cut the chain precisely in half.

Open up the attachment component of each ear wire with round-nose pliers and thread on a cable link.

Attach six teardrop beads to each length of chain, one per link and one in the attachment component of of the ear wire.

BEADS & CHARMS

12 aurora borealis glass teardrops embedded with wire, 6 x 10 mm

FINDINGS

2 in. (5.1 cm) of medium brass cable chain
2 brass French lever-back ear wires

TOOLS

Round-nose pliers
Cutting pliers

Favorite Finds

ANTIQUE BEADED FLOWERS

Years ago in France, I came upon a treasure trove of antique beaded flowers, handmade at the turn of the last century for the millinery trade. I've loved using these flowers in everything from jewelry design to small beaded tiaras. To incorporate them in jewelry designs, simply cut the wire down to 1 inch (2.5 cm) and roll the wire around the nose of round-nose pliers to create a closed loop. Use a jump ring to attach beaded flowers, leaves, or stamens onto chain or beaded jewelry. To attach beaded flowers to a tiara, don't cut the wire, but instead wrap it completely around the base of your headpiece. Wire can be easily hidden by wrapping a ribbon around the base of your headpiece.

FÉVRIER

LA SAINT VALENTIN

A Frenchman, the Duke of Orléans, is thought to have written the first love letters that later became Valentine's Day cards. In 1415, the Duke was taken as a prisoner to London; while imprisoned in the Tower, he is thought to have written love letters to his wife back in France. These are thought to be what became cartes d'amitiés, now known as French Valentine's Day cards.

Material Inspiration: dusty corals, old pinks, glass pearls, heart lockets, and cameos to inspire lovely jewelry.

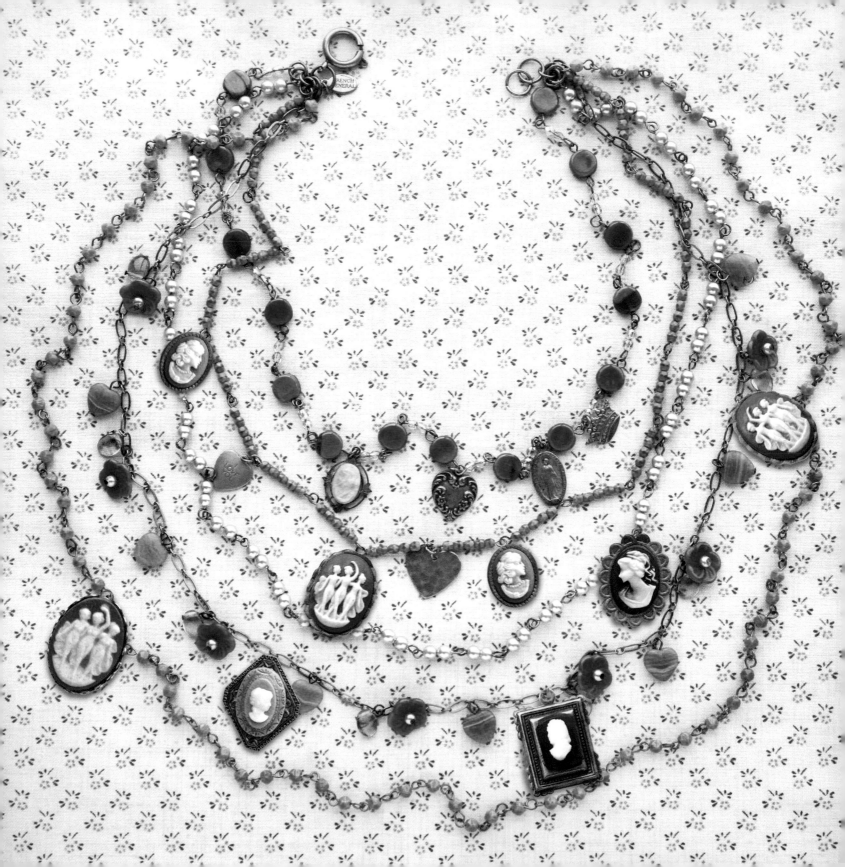

LA SAINT VALENTIN NECKLACE

DIRECTIONS

You'll make the longest strand first. Look for glass, plastic, or shell cameos and find bezels that they fit into. Glue cameos into bezels. Add the cameos to your jewelry designs by using a small jump ring.

STRAND NO. 5

Thread each bead onto an eye pin. Cut each eye pin and loop it onto another to form a rosary style chain. Open a 5-mm jump ring and connect it to one end of the chain, add the clasp onto the jump ring; then close it. Connect a 5-mm jump ring to the other end of the chain and close it. Finally, connect an 8-mm jump ring to this 5-mm jump ring—it will serve as the ring that connects to the clasp once all five strands are finished.

STRAND NO. 4

Thread each of the dime beads onto an eye pin. Thread two fire-polished beads onto each of 15 eye pins. Cut and loop each of the eye pins, linking them into a chain of alternating dime beads and fire-polished beads. Use the 3-mm jump rings to connect each of the charms, including the cameo, toward the center of the strand. Make sure they all hang facing the same way.

Connect a 5-mm jump ring to one end, connecting it to the 5-mm jump ring on the left side of strand no. 5 before closing it. Do the same at the other end of the necklace, connecting that end to the 5-mm jump ring on right side of strand no. 5. Lay out the beadwork so the charms face you. This will help as you continue to add strands to each other.

STRAND NO. 3

Thread five fire-polished bead onto each eye pin. Cut each eye pin and loop one to the next to form a rosary style chain. Using

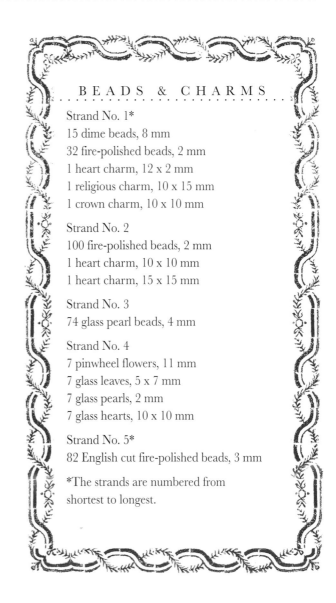

BEADS & CHARMS

Strand No. 1*
15 dime beads, 8 mm
32 fire-polished beads, 2 mm
1 heart charm, 12 x 2 mm
1 religious charm, 10 x 15 mm
1 crown charm, 10 x 10 mm

Strand No. 2
100 fire-polished beads, 2 mm
1 heart charm, 10 x 10 mm
1 heart charm, 15 x 15 mm

Strand No. 3
74 glass pearl beads, 4 mm

Strand No. 4
7 pinwheel flowers, 11 mm
7 glass leaves, 5 x 7 mm
7 glass pearls, 2 mm
7 glass hearts, 10 x 10 mm

Strand No. 5*
82 English cut fire-polished beads, 3 mm

*The strands are numbered from shortest to longest.

3-mm jump rings, connect each heart charm near the center of the strand. Remember to connect these in such a way that so they face forward like the charms on strand no. 5. Finish by connecting a 5-mm jump ring to one end; before closing it, attach it to the 5-mm jump ring on the left side of strand no. 5. Do the same on the other end: connect a 5-mm jump ring and before closing it, join it to the 5-mm jump ring on the right side of strand no. 5.

STRAND NO. 2

Thread two glass pearl onto each eye pin. Cut each eye pin and link them one to the next to form another rosary style chain similar to strand no. 5. Connect a 5-mm jump ring to one end; before closing it, connect it to the 5-mm jump ring on the left side of strand no. 1. Do the same on the other side of the strand: attach a 5-mm jump ring and connect it to the 5-mm jump ring on the right side of strand no. 5.

STRAND NO. 1

Thread each of the glass pearls onto a head pin, followed by a flower. Cut each wire down to $\frac{1}{4}$ in. (6 mm), bend the wire down at a 90° angle, and make a loop, attaching the flowers to the chain eight links apart. (To do this, start at the center link of the chain; then attach three flowers on one side, and three on the other.) Then thread each of the glass leaves onto a head pin and cut and loop each onto the chain right next to a flower. Thread each of the glass hearts onto a head pin; then cut and loop one onto the chain between every flower. Finish by connecting a 5-mm jump ring to one end of the strand; before closing it, attach it to the 5-mm jump ring on the left side of strand no. 1. Connect a 5-mm jump ring to the other end of the strand and attach it to the 5-mm jump ring on the right side of strand no. 1.

FINDINGS

Strand No. 1
30 brass eye pins, 1 inch (2.5 cm)
4 brass jump rings, 3 mm
2 brass jump rings, 5 mm

Strand No. 2
20 brass eye pins, 1 inch (2.5 cm)
2 brass jump rings, 3 mm
2 brass jump rings, 5 mm

Strand No. 3
37 brass eye pins, 1 inch (2.5 cm)
2 brass jump rings, 5 mm

Strand No. 4
21 brass head pins, 1 inch (2.5 cm)
2 brass jump rings, 5 mm
20 inches (50.8 cm) of small brass
  cable chain

Strand No. 5
82 brass eye pins, 1 inch (2.5 cm)
2 brass jump rings, 5 mm
1 brass jump ring, 8 mm
1 brass watch clasp, 12 mm

TOOLS

Round-nose pliers
Flat-nose pliers
Cutting pliers
Jewelry glue

HELPFUL TIPS

MAKING MULTIPLE-STRAND JEWELRY

My designs often start out as a one-strand necklace, but over time I continue to add on and eventually the necklace ends up being multiple strands...even though that wasn't the original intention! Making necklaces with multiple strands can take a lot of time, so instead of sitting down and expecting to finish a five- or six-strand necklace in one afternoon, consider making a two- or three-strand necklace and then add on more strands as you find the time.

CHARMING CHARMS

I tend to scoop up heart charms and beads whenever I see them, just so I have plenty to choose from when I make up my Valentine-inspired jewels. I also love including flowers in shades of pink and red to lend a romantic look to the jewelry. You can also add in pale pink silk ribbon to make the jewels seem a bit softer. Or make just a bracelet with a clasp, thread it through a length of silk ribbon 18 inches (45.7 cm) long, and then wear it as a necklace.

LA SAINT VALENTIN BRACELET

DIRECTIONS

Connect the watch clasp to one end of the chain using the 5-mm jump ring. Connect the 8-mm jump ring to the other end of the chain. Untwist the chain and lay it out with the clasp on the left—this will ensure that everything is being connected on the same side of the chain. Arrange the design of the bracelet in such a way as to balance out all of the beads with the charms.

Thread each of the glass pearls onto a head pin, followed by a flower. Cut the wire down to ¼ in. (6 mm), bend wire at a 90° angle, and loop the wire, attaching the flowers to the chain about an inch (2.5 cm) apart from each other. Thread each of the remaining beads onto a head pin, cut the wire, and loop each onto the chain. Use the 3-mm jump rings to connect each of the charms to the chain. For any embedded wire glass beads, cut the wire down to ¼ in. (6 mm) and loop it onto the chain.

LA SAINT VALENTIN EARRINGS

DIRECTIONS

Thread a glass pearl onto a head pin, followed by a flower. Cut the wire down to ¼ in. (6 mm), bend it at a 90° angle and make a loop. Thread a leaf bead onto a head pin, cut the wire and loop it. Use a jump ring to attach the flower bead and the leaf bead to the ear wire. Repeat to make a second earring.

BEADS & CHARMS

8 glass pearls, 2 mm
8 pinwheel flowers, 11 mm
6 dime beads, 8 mm
8 teardrops, 5 x 8 mm
7 flat ovals, 5 x 8 mm
3 wire-embedded beads, 10 mm
1 heart bead, 15 x 15 mm
5 small heart charms

FINDINGS

30 brass head pins, 1 inch (2.5 cm)
5 brass jump rings, 3 mm
1 brass jump ring, 5 mm
1 brass jump ring, 8 mm
1 brass watch clasp, 12 mm
7½ in. (19 cm) of medium brass cable chain

TOOLS

Round-nose pliers
Flat-nose pliers
Cutting pliers
Jewelry glue

BEADS & CHARMS

2 glass pearls, 2 mm
2 pinwheel flowers, 11 mm
2 glass leaves, 5 x 7 mm

FINDINGS

4 brass head pins, 1 inch (2.5 cm)
2 brass jump rings, 3 mm
2 brass French lever-back ear wires

TOOLS

Round-nose pliers
Cutting pliers

FAVORITE FINDS

CAMEOS

Cameos enchanted Napoleon, who wore one to his own wedding and founded a school in Paris to teach the art of cameo carving to young apprentices. While hunting for beads in Providence, I came across a basement full of old glass and shell cameos. I dug around for hours to find the perfect bezels for the cameos and eventually found a box full of cameo lockets as well. I still look for cameos, but they tend to be few and far between. I treasure the ones I have for my special jewelry pieces.

MARS

LE PRINTEMPS

The French word for spring or springtime is printemps. The Springtime in France is one of the most beautiful, colorful seasons, from the first weeks of March to the warmer month of May. Many flowers come into bloom in the early season of spring: hyacinth, iris, ranunculus, and especially snowdrops. Additional flowers that bloom in France throughout the month of March include: the wood violet, cowslip, common primrose, lily of the valley, forget me not, and wild daffodil.

Material Inspiration: pale blue, barely-there pink, mossy green, and lavender flowers, ladybugs, and botanical charms to create a garden-inspired palette.

HELPFUL TIPS

LAYERING FLOWERS

Create fantasy flowers by layering flat flowers with other types of petals and stamens. Thread a head pin through the top of the smallest flower first, then the medium size, and finally the largest flower. Bend the head pin 90° to secure all the beads on the head pin. Using your round-nose pliers, simply wrap a loop and connect the component to the chain. The flowers will lie flat if you're sure to bend the wire 90° before looping the wire closed.

LE PRINTEMPS NECKLACE

DIRECTIONS

Connect the watch clasp to one end of the chain by using your flat-nose pliers and a 5-mm jump ring. Connect an 8-mm jump ring to the other end of the chain. Arrange the chain with the clasp on the left side and keep it that way the whole time you're making the necklace—this will ensure that everything is being connected on the same side of the chain.

Layer the flower beads onto the head pins, always starting by threading on the smallest bead first, then the medium, and finally the largest petal or flower. Lay out the necklace design by arranging the flowers and leaves in a symmetrical fashion. For my necklace, I started in the middle and developed a pattern up the left side of the necklace and then up the right side.

Once you have a pattern laid out, string any unthreaded beads onto a head pin. (Anything with a hole, like a charm or the Lucite leaves, will be connected to the chain with a 5-mm jump ring.) Cut down each head pin to ½ in. (1.3 cm) above the bead. Loop each wire with your round-nose pliers and connect the dangle to the chain. Be sure to connect the next bead, charm, or dangle along the bottom of the chain—follow the pattern from the first bead— so that the dangles and charms won't twist. Continue to loop head pins and connect jump rings onto chain until you're finished using all of the beads and charms.

BEADS & CHARMS

10 flat Lucite flowers, 20 mm
10 Lucite or glass daisy petals, 10 to 15 mm
10 glass baby bell flowers, 4 x 6 mm
6 glass trumpet flowers, 5 x 8 mm
5 glass ladybugs, 9 x 7 mm
9 glass leaves, 9 x 7 mm
8 glass leaves, 8 x 10 mm
3 Lucite leaves, 15 x 20 mm
9 brass garden-inspired charms, 10 to 25 mm

FINDINGS

38 brass head pins, 1 inch (2.5 cm)
13 brass jump rings, 5 mm
1 brass jump ring, 8 mm
1 brass watch clasp, 12 mm
24 inches (61 cm) of small brass cable chain

TOOLS

Round-nose pliers
Flat-nose pliers
Cutting pliers

FRICATION FRANÇAISE

Armand Pain
PARIS, 55 Rue ... Ménilmontant, 55 PARIS.

HELPFUL TIPS

SPRINGTIME JEWELRY

Look for old glass flowers and leaves of all shapes and sizes. Many glass flowers and leaves have holes so they can be attached with jump rings. Brass charms of insects, including bees, beetles, ladybugs, and butterflies, as well as birds and nests, all add a whimsical look to springtime-inspired jewelry.

LE PRINTEMPS BRACELET

DIRECTIONS

Connect the watch clasp to one end of the chain by using the flat-nose pliers and a 5-mm jump ring. Connect an 8-mm jump ring to the other end of the chain. Arrange the chain with the clasp on the left side and keep it that way the entire time you make the bracelet—this will ensure that everything is being connected on the same side of the chain.

Layer the flower beads onto the head pins, always start by threading on the smallest bead first, then the medium, and finally the largest petal or flower. Lay out your bracelet design by arranging the flowers and leaves in a symmetrical fashion.

Once you have a pattern laid out, thread all beads onto a head pin. (Anything with a hole, like a charm or the Lucite leaves, will be connected with a 5-mm jump ring.) Cut down the head pin wire to ½ in. (1.3 cm) above the bead. Loop each wire with your round-nose pliers and connect the dangle to the chain. Be sure to connect the next bead, charm, or dangle along the bottom of the chain—following the pattern from the first bead—to keep your beads and charms from twisting. Continue to loop the head pins and connect jump rings onto the chain until you've attached all of your beads and charms.

LE PRINTEMPS EARRINGS

DIRECTIONS

Layer the flower beads onto two of the head pins, always start by threading on the smallest bead first, then the medium, and finally the largest petal or flower. Cut down the wire to ½ in. (1.3 cm) above the bead. Connect these dangles to the ear wires by looping the wire and attaching it to the small ring at the front of the ear wire. Thread two glass leaves onto two different head pins, cut the wire ½ in. (1.3 cm) above each bead, and loop the dangles onto the small ring on one of the ear wires. Repeat to finish the other earring.

BEADS & CHARMS

3 flat Lucite flowers, 20 mm
2 Lucite leaves, 12 x 10 mm
3 Lucite or glass daisy petals, 10 to 15 mm
3 glass baby bell flowers, 4 x 6 mm
6 glass trumpet flowers, 5 x 8 mm
6 glass ladybugs, 9 x 7 mm
4 glass leaves, 9 x 7 mm
4 glass leaves, 8 x 10 mm
4 brass garden-inspired charms, 10 to 25 mm

FINDINGS

23 brass head pins, 1 inch (2.5 cm)
5 brass jump rings, 5 mm
1 brass jump ring, 8 mm
1 brass watch clasp, 12 mm
7 inches (17.8 cm) of small brass cable chain

TOOLS

Round-nose pliers
Flat-nose pliers
Cutting pliers

MATERIALS

2 flat Lucite flowers, 20 mm
2 Lucite or glass daisy petals, 10 to 15 mm
2 glass trumpet flowers, 5 x 8 mm
4 glass leaves, 9 x 7 mm

FINDINGS

6 brass headpins, 1 inch (2.5 cm)
2 brass French lever-back ear wires

TOOLS

Round-nose pliers
Cutting pliers

Favorite Finds

LUCITE FLOWERS & LEAVES

For years, I would have nothing to do with plastic or Lucite beads…and then I found a supplier who offered such beautiful shades of Lucite flowers, petals, and leaves that I couldn't say no! Lucite flowers and leaves were made in Germany in the 1960s and '70s, and they're still being reproduced today due to popular demand. They're perfect for clustered earrings because they're light as a feather, and they can easily be dyed your favorite color by letting them sit in a bath of fabric dye.

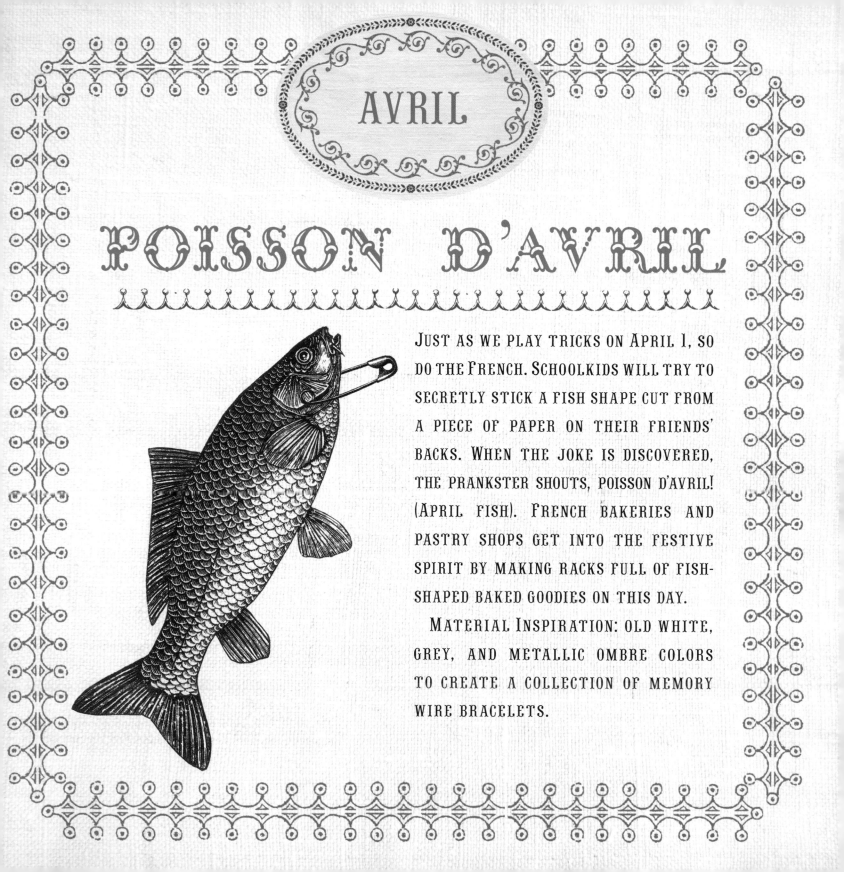

AVRIL

POISSON D'AVRIL

Just as we play tricks on April 1, so do the French. Schoolkids will try to secretly stick a fish shape cut from a piece of paper on their friends' backs. When the joke is discovered, the prankster shouts, poisson d'avril! (April fish). French bakeries and pastry shops get into the festive spirit by making racks full of fish-shaped baked goodies on this day.

Material Inspiration: old white, grey, and metallic ombre colors to create a collection of memory wire bracelets.

HELPFUL TIPS

USING MEMORY WIRE

Memory wire is designed to always retain its original shape. When making individual bangles, be sure to cut the wire at least 1 in. (2.5 cm) longer than your required measurement, so it overlaps on each end; this will prevent the bangles from falling off your wrist. Making a loop at both ends of the wire is the best way to secure beads on a bracelet. You can also find memory wire in ring size, which is fun to use to make beaded rings. When making a memory-wire ring for your finger, gluing two or three seed beads on either end, rather than looping the ends, is the best way to secure the beads.

POISSON D'AVRIL BRACELET

DIRECTIONS

Using the round-nose pliers, make a loop on one end of the wire. Thread beads onto wire, and when you get to the end of the wire, leave ¼ in. (6 mm) of the wire empty and loop that section of wire closed. Repeat with different beads to make up a set of bangles.

POISSON D'AVRIL CUFF

DIRECTIONS

Using the round-nose pliers, make a loop on one end of the wire. Thread the ribbon, alternating with pearls, onto the wire. When you get to the end of the wire, leave ¼ in. (6 mm) of the wire empty and loop it closed.

BEADS

85 crystal beads, 3 mm
120 bugle beads, 1 mm
170 seed beads, 1 mm

FINDINGS

7 ½ in. (19 cm) of memory wire for each bangle

TOOLS

Round-nose pliers
Cutting pliers

BEADS

54 glass pearls, 10 mm

FINDINGS

20 inches (50.8 cm) of memory wire
36 inches (91.4 cm) of gray linen ribbon, 10 mm

TOOLS

Round-nose pliers
Cutting pliers

HELPFUL TIPS

USING YOUR STASH

Memory wire bracelets are the perfect piece of jewelry to use all of your mixed beads. Separate out your beads to make up fun patterns in color palettes, size, and texture. When making a multiwrap cuff, I usually make up patterns with six to ten beads to create small sections of beaded jewels. While it creates a single bracelet, it gives the illusion of multiple bracelets stacked together. Another design idea is working with beads of a similar shade, like I did with the seed bead bangles. Choose a color of seed bead and then select a shade darker and shade lighter than that to create an ombre effect when they're worn together.

POISSON D'AVRIL BRACELET

DIRECTIONS

Using the round-nose pliers, make a loop on one end of the wire. Thread beads and buttons onto the wire. When you reach the end of the wire, leave ¼ in. (6 mm) of the wire empty and loop the wire closed.

Memory wire is a flexible coil wire that comes in pre-formed bracelet, necklace and ring shapes and accepts a wide range of bead sizes.

BEADS

The true joy of this bracelet is that you can use all materials you already have. Dig through your old bead and button stash and separate it into color palettes: red, orange, pink, yellow, and then blue, green, purple, turquoise or even white, gray, tan, and pearl. You should gather enough beads to cover approximately 40 inches (1 m) of memory wire.

FINDINGS

40 in. (1 m) of memory wire

TOOLS

Round-nose pliers
Cutting pliers

Favorite Finds

GLASS PEARLS

I use a lot of old glass pearls made in Japan and Europe in the 1930s and '40s. Depending on exposure to the elements, the pearl coating will either be in perfect shape, coating the entire bead, or chipping, which will continue to flake off with more wear. Try to avoid chipping glass pearls, unless you like the look of the bare milk glass underneath. Old glass pearls can be found in many colors, my favorite being couture color, a creamy, natural luster color. I also love the matte and shiny white glass pearls. When you find a stash of these old glass pearls, be sure to add them to your collection! They're rare and becoming harder to find.

MAI

LA MARIÉE

WHILE JUNE IS THE BIG MONTH FOR WEDDINGS IN THE UNITED STATES, THE MOST POPULAR TIME FOR NUPTIALS IN FRANCE IS MAY. WEDDINGS USUALLY TAKE PLACE ON SATURDAY AFTERNOONS, TO ALLOW FOR AN ELABORATE RECEPTION AND SUPPER AFTERWARD. IN SMALLER FRENCH TOWNS, THE GROOM MAY MEET HIS FIANCÉE AT HER HOME ON THE DAY OF THE WEDDING AND ESCORT HER TO THE CHAPEL WHERE THE CEREMONY IS BEING HELD. AS THE COUPLE PROCEEDS TO THE CHAPEL, CHILDREN WILL STRETCH LONG WHITE RIBBONS ACROSS THE ROAD WHICH THE BRIDE WILL CUT AS SHE PASSES.

MATERIAL INSPIRATION: OLD MOTHER-OF-PEARL, GLASS PEARLS, AND SILK RIBBON FOR A VINTAGE-INSPIRED WEDDING SET.

L'EPINGLE ROYALE

HELPFUL TIPS

BRIDAL JEWELRY

When making bridal jewelry, try to use an old charm or family memento that will resonate with the couple. Pearls are always a welcome material, but often the bride will want something that makes a statement and adds a bit of color. Think about using pale blue crystals mixed with pearls for a twist on the saying "something old, something new, something borrowed, something blue."

LA MARIÉE NECKLACE

Connect the watch clasp to one end of the chain with a 5-mm jump ring. Connect an 8-mm jump ring to the other end of the chain. Using a beading needle, thread the silk ribbon in and out of the cable chain. Knot it off at both ends, leaving a tail of at least 10 in. (25.4 cm) on each side. Thread all beads onto head pins, including any buttons that might also be attached with a head pin. If the hole on the button is too wide for the headpin, add a small 3-mm aurora borealis bead. Cut and loop all head pins and connect them to the chain on the small cable links.

Connect all crystal and mother-of-pearl buttons to the larger cable links using 5-mm jump rings. The design of this necklace, unlike most other necklaces, allows for beads to be linked on either side of the cable chain without concern about whether they lay flat.

BEADS AND CHARMS

25 glass pearls, 10 mm
3 mother-of-pearl button, 20 mm
3 mother-of-pearl buttons, 10 mm
5 crystal buttons, 12 mm
5 crystal buttons, 5 mm
16 aurora borealis beads, 3 mm

FINDINGS

41 brass head pins, 1 in. (2.5 cm)
17 brass jump rings, 5 mm
1 brass jump ring, 8 mm
21 in. (53.3 cm) of medium brass cable chain
1 brass watch clasp, 15 mm
44 in. (1.1 m) of taupe silk ribbon, 1¼ in. (3.2 cm) wide

TOOLS

Round-nose pliers
Flat-nose pliers
Cutting pliers

HELPFUL TIPS

CREATING A WHITE PALETTE

When pulling together beads for a bridal palette, consider using all shades of natural white, including opal, pearl, opaque, moonstone, and mother-of-pearl. A good blend of all these shades will make a beautiful color scheme that reads with more depth than just plain white.

LA MARIÉE BRACELETS

DIRECTIONS

Cut a piece of elastic thread 8 in. (20.3 cm) long. Tie a triple knot at one end. Thread on two to four crystals and then thread on a button. Continue adding this pattern of crystals and then a button until you have at least 6 to 7 in. (15.2–17.8 cm) of materials. Carefully wrap the elastic with its beads and buttons around your wrist to see if it's the desired length. When it is, tie the ends together close to the beads with a triple knot; drop a bit of glue on it. Set aside to dry for at least 15 minutes.

LA MARIÉE EARRINGS

DIRECTIONS

Thread an eye pin through a 3-mm glass pearl bead, cut the wire, and connect it to the ear wire's loop. Thread an eye pin through a 4-mm glass pearl, cut the wire, and loop it onto the pearl's eye pin. Thread an eye pin through a milk glass bead, cut the wire, and loop it onto the glass pearl's eye pin. Thread an eye pin through the 8-mm mother-of-pearl bead, cut the wire, and loop it onto the milk glass bead's loop. Thread a head pin through a 12-mm glass pearl, cut the wire, and loop it onto the mother-of-pearl bead. Repeat to make a second earring.

BEADS, FOR EACH

20 mother-of-pearl buttons, 10–20 mm
30 to 40 crystal bicones, 4 mm

FINDINGS

Elastic thread

TOOLS

Scissors
Jewelry glue

MATERIALS

2 glass pearl beads, 3 mm
2 glass pearl beads, 4 mm
2 milk glass beads, 6 mm
2 mother of pearl beads, 8 mm
2 glass pearl beads, 12 mm

FINDINGS

8 brass eye pins, 1 in. (2.5 cm)
2 brass head pins, 1 in. (2.5 cm)
2 brass fishhook ear wires

TOOLS

Round nose pliers
Cutting pliers

La Côte St André le 12 Juillet 1894.

Favorite Finds

· · · · · · · · · · · · · · · · ·

MERCURY GLASS

In the early 1800s, blown glass beads were lined with a solution that contained mercury. By the mid-1800s, the lining had been switched to silver nitrate, sugar, and water. These beads came in all shapes, textures, and sizes and were primarily used to embellish clothing. Mercury glass beads are a special item to use in jewelry design, but they're extremely fragile and must be handled with care.

JUIN

LES FRUITS

At all of the local farmer's markets in France throughout the summer months, you will find a great variety of fruit, including: raspberries, strawberries, red currants, apricots, cherries, lemons, melons, white and yellow peaches, and plums of all shades. The fruit is piled high and ripe for the picking. Don't forget your market basket!

Material Inspiration: bright cherry reds, lemon yellows, and orange glass poppies blend together for a fresh palette for summer.

LES FRUITS NECKLACE

DIRECTIONS

STRAND NO. 1

Connect the watch clasp to the left side of the chain using a 5-mm jump ring. Connect a 5-mm jump ring to the opposite side of the chain and then connect the 8-mm jump ring to it. Lay out the chain with the clasp on the left side—this will ensure that everything is being connected on the same side of the chain. Divide the English cut beads into seven sets of three. Thread a set of three beads onto a head pin, cut the wire down to ¼ in. (6 mm) and make a loop. Repeat with the remaining piles. Slide three English cut beads onto a 5-mm jump ring and connect the jump ring to the chain. (To do this, start at the centermost link, then attach three sets 1 in. [2.5 cm]—or three links—apart on one side; attach the three remaining sets three links apart on the other side.) Arrange your flower, fruit, and leaf beads in a pattern along the edge of the chain. Thread each bead in turn onto a head pin, cut the wire down to ¼ in. (6 mm), and loop it onto the chain. For embedded wire beads, simply cut wire down to ¼ in. (6 mm) and connect it to the chain.

STRAND NO. 2

Thread a head pin through each fire-polished bead, cut the wire down to ¼ in. (6 mm), and loop it closed. Attach two of these components to each 5-mm jump ring and connect them directly to the chain. Continue connecting these clusters about an inch (2.5 cm) apart on the chain. For more even spacing, count the links on the chain between each cluster. Thread an eye pin through each leaf bead and connect one right beside each cluster of fire-polished beads on the chain. Finish by connecting a 5-mm jump ring to one end of the chain; before closing it, attach it to the 5-mm jump ring on the left side of strand no. 1. Do the same on the other side of the necklace: connect a 5-mm jump ring to the end and before closing, attach it to the 5-mm jump ring on the right side of strand no. 1.

BEADS

Strand No. 1*
4 wire-embedded fruits, 10 mm
7 wire-embedded glass flowers, 14 mm
4 wire-embedded glass flowers, 17 mm
19 glass leaves, 9 x 7 mm
21 English cut or fire-polished beads, 7 mm

Strand No. 2
28 English cut or fire-polished beads, 7 mm
14 glass leaves, 9 x 7 mm

*This is the shorter strand.

FINDINGS

Strand No. 1
40 brass head pins, 1 inch (2.5 cm)
10 brass jump rings, 5 mm
1 brass jump ring, 8 mm
1 brass watch clasp, 12 mm
20 inches (50.8 cm) of medium brass cable chain

Strand No. 2
42 brass head pins, 1 inch (2.5 cm)
16 brass jump rings, 5 mm
25 inches (63.5 cm) of small brass cable chain

TOOLS

Round-nose pliers
Flat-nose pliers
Cutting pliers

GLASS FRUIT

I'm always on the lookout for hand-blown glass fruit beads. If I don't happen to have any on hand, I improvise with old cherry red, orange, yellow, and purple fire-polished beads. Thread a bunch of beads onto head pins and then connect them to a small cable chain, going lighter at the bottom and then heavier at the top. This makes a great cluster of grapes. Add in a green leaf here and there to make the design resemble a vine.

LES FRUITS BRACELET

DIRECTIONS

Connect the watch clasp to one end of the chain using a 5-mm jump ring. Connect the 8-mm jump ring to the other end of the chain. Untwist the chain and lay it out with the clasp on the left side—this will ensure that you connect everything on the same side of the chain.

Divide the English-cut beads into five sets of three. Add a leaf bead to each set. Thread each bead with a head pin, cut the wire down to ¼ in. (6 mm) and make a loop. Open a 5-mm jump ring, and slip on one set of three English-cut beads and one leaf. Connect this jump ring to the chain. Continue connecting these clusters about an inch (2.5 cm) apart on the chain. For more spacing, count the links on the chain between each cluster.

Arrange the remaining beads along the length of the chain. Attach them to the chain with head pins, or for the wire-embedded fruits and flowers, simply cut the wire down to ¼ in. (6 mm) and make a loop.

MATERIALS

3 wire-embedded glass fruits, 11 mm
5 wire-embedded glass flowers, 14 mm
2 wire-embedded glass flowers, 17 mm
15 English cut or fire-polished beads, 7 mm
10 glass leaves, 9 x 7 mm

FINDINGS

22 brass head pins, 1 inch (2.5 cm)
6 brass jump rings, 5 mm
1 brass jump ring, 8 mm
1 brass watch clasp, 12 mm
7½ in. (19 cm) of medium brass cable chain

TOOLS

Round-nose pliers
Flat-nose pliers

LES FRUITS EARRINGS

DIRECTIONS

Divide the beads evenly and set half of them aside. Cut the small cable chain wire into two equal pieces. Open the loop of an ear wire and connect one piece of chain to it. Thread an English-cut bead onto a head pin, cut the wire, and loop it onto loose end link of the chain. Continue attaching English-cut beads in this same manner, evenly arranged along the bottom two-thirds of the chain, fastening them onto opposite sides of chain to give the drops some visual weight.

Thread a glass leaf onto a head pin, cut the wire, and loop it onto the topmost link of the chain. Attach the rest of the leaf beads in this same manner along the top third of the chain, connecting them onto opposite sides of chain. Also attach one to the loop in the ear wire. Repeat to make the second earring.

MATERIALS

12 English cut or fire-polished beads, 7 mm
6 glass leaves, 9 x 7 mm

FINDINGS

24 brass head pins, 1 inch (2.5 cm)
3 inches (7.6 cm) of small brass cable chain
2 brass French lever-back ear wires

TOOLS

Round-nose pliers
Flat-nose pliers
Cutting pliers

Favorite Finds

··

WIRE-EMBEDDED GLASS

I love finding wire-embedded glass leaves, fruits, and flowers. Made in Murano, Italy, throughout the early part of the twentieth century, these delicate glass charms are easily used by cutting down the wire and looping it onto a piece of chain. Be careful not to put too much stress on the wire as it can easily break or snap off where the wire meets the top of the glass. When you find these beauties, scoop them all up—they're quite rare and disappearing fast!

JUILLET

LA FÊTE NATIONALE

France commemorates the beginning of the French Revolution on July 14. While we may call it Bastille Day, the French don't. For them it's quite simply le quatorze juillet, July 14, just as we call our Independence Day the Fourth of July.

Material Inspiration: old red, antique gold, and hematite with splashes of rhinestones and leather for a bit of the unexpected.

HELPFUL TIPS

WORKING WITH LEATHER

Look for old, well-worn leather gloves at flea markets and second-hand stores. If you find gloves that are worn and dirty, you can give them a fresh, new life by tossing them into the washing machine—just be sure to air dry them. Look for gloves with delicate edging that adds to the jewelry design, or use a pinking shear to cut a decorative edge. If the leather is soft enough, you should be able to sew through it easily with a needle and thread.

LA FÊTE NATIONALE NECKLACE

DIRECTIONS

Using pinking shears or embroidery scissors, cut a scalloped edge on one side of the leather. Thread the needle and sew on seed beads to accent the edge of the leather. Gather the opposite edge of the leather and stitch it to the back of the shoe clip.

Embellish the top of the shoe clip by gluing the crystal to its center and stitching small brass torse around the crystal.

Cut the chain into four equal pieces. Using a 5-mm jump ring, connect two pieces of chain to one side of the shoe clip. Repeat on the opposite side. Connect the lobster claw to two pieces of the chain with a 3-mm jump ring. Connect a 3-mm jump ring to the other end of the chain and add on the 8-mm jump ring as your closure ring.

MATERIALS

17 brass torse, or textured brass beads, 2 mm
11 red crystal seed beads, 1 mm
66 crystal seed beads, 1 mm
1 flat-back crystal, 5 mm
1 antique hematite shoe clip, 40 mm
4 x 2 in. (10.2 x 5.1 cm) of kid leather

FINDINGS

2 brass jump rings, 5 mm
2 black-ox jump rings, 3 mm
1 black-ox jump ring, 8 mm
1 black-ox lobster-claw clasp, 10 mm
28 in. (71.1 cm) of black-ox small
    cable chain

TOOLS

Sewing needle
Sewing thread
Pinking shears or fine embroidery scissors
Flat-nose pliers
Cutting pliers

HELPFUL TIPS

FESTIVE JEWELRY PALETTE

Working with red, white, and blue can be limiting if you only use one shade of each color. Consider using different shades of this patriotic palette—like ruby and cherry red, Montana and sapphire blue, and pearl and crystal for white. Sometimes a small accent of color does the trick with festive jewelry and allows you to wear it all year long.

LA FÊTE NATIONALE BRACELET

DIRECTIONS

Arrange the rhinestone strip along the center of the leather strip. Tack it down every $1/4$ in. (6 mm) with needle and thread by sewing through both the rhinestone strip and the leather strip. Knot off. With a new sewing thread, sew the rondelle beads to the center of the rhinestone strip, sewing through the leather. Knot off with a triple knot. You can attach the grommet at the end of the leather strap with a hammer, but

I usually take my leather pieces to a shoe repair or leather shop and have them attach the grommet with a foot-press attachment machine. You can attach the buckle at the end of the leather strap with a grommet and a hammer

LA FÊTE NATIONALE EARRINGS

DIRECTIONS

Glue the cabochons into their respective bezels and set them aside to dry. Using round-nose pliers, thread an eye pin with the 2 mm hematite crystal bead, cut and loop to one bezel.

Open the opposite side of the eye pin and connect to second bezel. The bead serves as the connector. Repeat to make second earring.

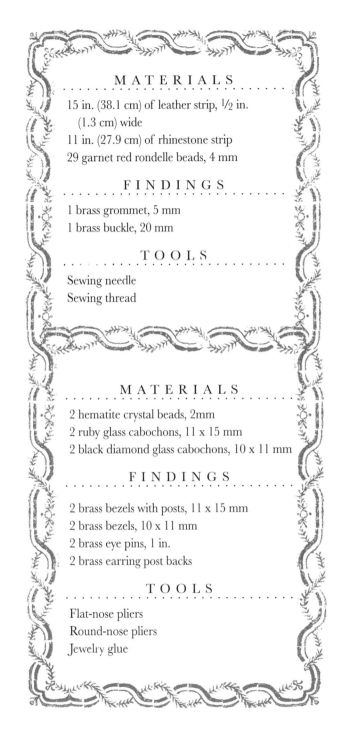

MATERIALS

15 in. (38.1 cm) of leather strip, $1/2$ in. (1.3 cm) wide
11 in. (27.9 cm) of rhinestone strip
29 garnet red rondelle beads, 4 mm

FINDINGS

1 brass grommet, 5 mm
1 brass buckle, 20 mm

TOOLS

Sewing needle
Sewing thread

MATERIALS

2 hematite crystal beads, 2mm
2 ruby glass cabochons, 11 x 15 mm
2 black diamond glass cabochons, 10 x 11 mm

FINDINGS

2 brass bezels with posts, 11 x 15 mm
2 brass bezels, 10 x 11 mm
2 brass eye pins, 1 in.
2 brass earring post backs

TOOLS

Flat-nose pliers
Round-nose pliers
Jewelry glue

FAVORITE FINDS

· ·

VINTAGE RHINESTONES

While hunting for treasures at flea markets or second-hand stores, keep your eye open for old rhinestone or paste jewelry. Popular during the 1930s and '40s, rhinestone jewelry adds a bit of sparkle to jewelry projects while giving it some Old World glamour. Oftentimes, stones are missing from the settings, but you may be able to salvage one good earring, charm, or chain. I never worry about cutting up old jewelry if I can give it a new life.

AOÛT

LES GRANDES VACANCES

French workers have the luxury of a month of paid vacation. Roughly half of French citizens take their vacations during the months of either July or August, so a good part of the country shuts down. To relax and rejuvenate, people escape the cities and go to the mountains, to the country, or to the sea.

Material Inspiration: clear aqua, pearls, white opal glass, and sea foam beads mixed with shells from the sea to create a set of jewelry to take on holiday.

MIXING AQUA COLORS

One of my favorite palettes is the soft colors of the sea—pale aqua, sea foam green, and dusty turquoise. For some reason, unknown to me, these are also some of the hardest colors to find while digging for old beads. When mixing this warm, aqua palette, I often improvise with a variety of similar colors. I include any shade of pale green and blue, as well as white opal and aurora borealis (AB) beads for a soft shimmer and glow.

LES GRANDES VACANCES NECKLACE

DIRECTIONS

Using a toothpick and jewelry glue that dries crystal clear, attach a flat-back pearl inside one shell charms and embellish the outside of the other shell charm with flat-back crystals and small pearls. Let dry completely.

Cut the chain into two pieces 6 inches (15.2 cm) long and eight pieces 1 in. (2.5 cm) long. Using the eye pins, make 10 segments each consisting of one pearl on the first eye pin, a brass torse bead with aqua bead and another torse bead on the next eye pin, and then a pearl on a third eye pin.

Link half of these bead segments with 1-inch chain pieces between them, then at one end attach one of the 6-in. (15.2 cm) pieces of chain, which will be the back of the necklace. Repeat to connect the remaining bead segments into a second, identical length.

Connect the watch clasp to one of the 6-in. (15.2 cm) pieces of chain using a 5-mm jump ring. Connect an 8-mm jump ring to the other the 6-in. (15.2 cm) piece of chain, as your closure.

Connect the two pieces of chain at what will be the center of the necklace by attaching the last two aqua beads together using a 5-mm jump ring. Thread head pins onto seafoam beads and connect these to that same 5-mm jump ring. Using a 3-mm jump ring, connect the two shell charms together to make a complete shell, to the 5-mm jump ring.

BEADS AND CHARMS

10 aqua beads, 10 mm
2 seafoam beads, 13 mm
20 brass torse or textured brass beads, 2 mm
18 pearl beads, 3 mm
2 shell charms, 40 mm
1 flat-back pearl, 10 mm

To embellish the shell charm:
36 flat-back crystals and pearls, 2–4 mm

FINDINGS

28 brass eye pins, 1 in. (2.5 cm)
3 brass head pins, 1 in. (2.5 cm)
1 brass jump ring, 3 mm
2 brass jump rings, 5 mm
2 brass jump rings, 8 mm
1 brass watch clasp, 12 mm
20 in. (50.8 cm) of small brass cable chain

TOOLS

Round-nose pliers
Flat-nose pliers
Cutting pliers
Jewelry glue
Toothpick

HELPFUL TIPS

CRYSTAL CABOCHONS

Using small crystal chatons and cabochons can give your jewelry a little bit of sparkle without overwhelming the whole piece. Choose soft colors such as pale topaz, light aqua, and champagne. They blend together perfectly and give almost an ombre effect when used together. Use a touch of glue that dries crystal clear to hold these tiny gems on glass beads, shells, or even brass charms.

LES GRANDES VACANCES BRACELET

DIRECTIONS

Glue all rhinestone and pearl embellishments to the beads or charms, then set them aside to dry.

Connect the watch clasp to one end of the chain using a 5-mm jump ring. Connect the 8-mm jump ring to the other end of the chain.

Due to the amount of beads and charms in this bracelet, there's no need to connect them to just one side of the chain. This bracelet wears better when charms and beads are connected to both the lower and upper part of the cable chain. Thread the bead cap, larger beads, and accent beads onto some head pins. Cut and loop them onto cable chain. Add several beads together onto head pins to make small, jewel-like bead charms. Attach all shell and brass charms using the 5-mm jump rings.

MATERIALS

2 shells, 14 mm
1 shell, 28 mm
1 shell, 21 mm
4 shell-shaped beads, 12 x 14 mm
10 small pearl beads, 3 mm
3 round turquoise beads, 8 mm
4 large pearl beads, 8 mm
14 moonstone beads, 6 mm
6 flat shell beads, 12 mm
3 flat-back crystals, 4 mm
1 flat-back oyster pearl, 6 mm
5 aqua beads, 10 mm
5 square green beads, 4 mm
3 flat white beads, 12 x 7 mm
5 faceted white beads, 4 mm
18 brass torse or textured brass beads, 2 mm
1 shell-shaped brass charm, 18 mm
1 shell-shaped brass charm, 20 mm

FINDINGS

3 brass bead caps, 8 mm
11 brass bead caps, 5 mm
38 brass head pins, 1 inch (2.5 cm)
1 brass jump ring, 8 mm
12 brass jump rings, 5 mm
1 brass watch clasp, 12 mm
7 1/2 inches (19 cm) of medium brass cable chain

TOOLS

Flat-nose pliers
Round-nose pliers
Cutting pliers
Jewelry glue

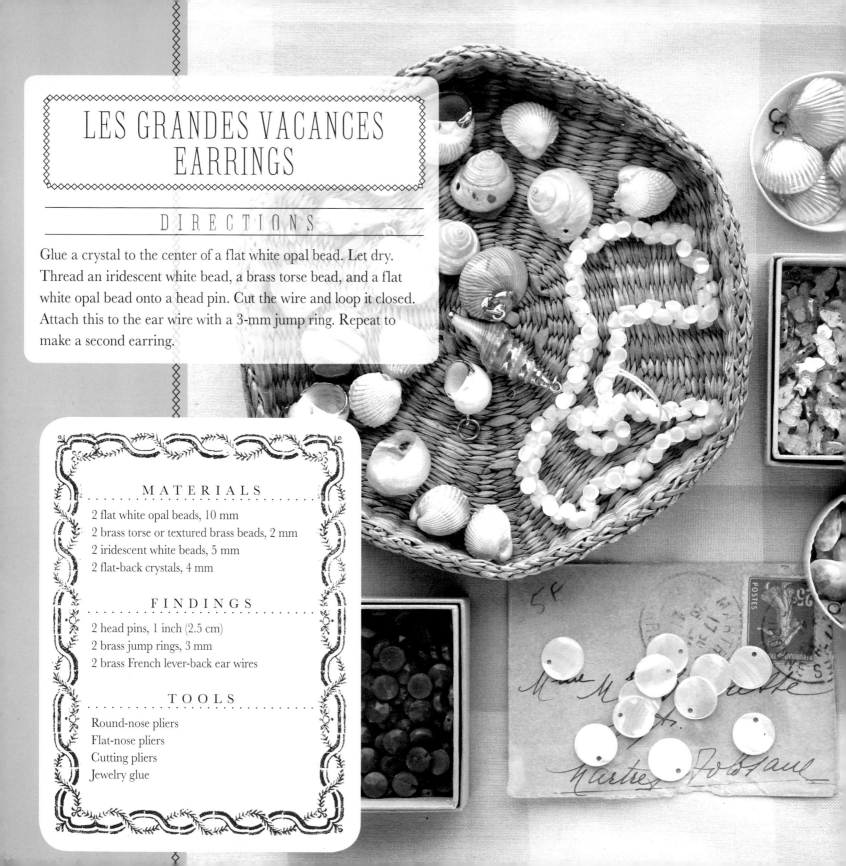

LES GRANDES VACANCES EARRINGS

DIRECTIONS

Glue a crystal to the center of a flat white opal bead. Let dry.
Thread an iridescent white bead, a brass torse bead, and a flat
white opal bead onto a head pin. Cut the wire and loop it closed.
Attach this to the ear wire with a 3-mm jump ring. Repeat to
make a second earring.

MATERIALS

2 flat white opal beads, 10 mm
2 brass torse or textured brass beads, 2 mm
2 iridescent white beads, 5 mm
2 flat-back crystals, 4 mm

FINDINGS

2 head pins, 1 inch (2.5 cm)
2 brass jump rings, 3 mm
2 brass French lever-back ear wires

TOOLS

Round-nose pliers
Flat-nose pliers
Cutting pliers
Jewelry glue

FAVORITE FINDS

LA CIGALE ET LA FOURMI
Il faut economiser dans la jeunesse pour en profiter dans la vieillesse.

LE SAVETIER ET LE FINANCIER.
L'argent ne fait pas le bonheur.

LE POT DE TERRE ET LE POT DE FER.
Ne nous associons qu'avec nos égaux.

LE CHIEN ET LE LOUP
Un petit chez soi vaut mieux qu'un grand chez les autres.

LE CHÊNE ET LE ROSEAU.
Le petit plie et se relève le grand résiste et tombe.

LA LAITIERE ET LE POT AU LAIT
Ne bâtissons pas de chateaux en Espagne.

LE RENARD ET LES RAISINS.
Il ne faut pas médire de ce que l'on ne peut posséder.

LE RAT ET L'HUITRE.
Tel est pris qui croyait prendre.

LE LIÈVRE ET LA TORTUE.
Rien ne sert de courir il faut partir à point.

LE LOUP ET L'AGNEAU.
Parfois la raison du plus fort est la meilleure.

LE LOUP, LA CHÈVRE ET LE CHEVREAU.
Prudence est mère de sureté.

LE PETIT POISSON ET LE PÊCHEUR.
Un tiens vaut mieux que deux tu l'auras.

LES GRENOUILLES QUI DEMANDENT UN ROI.
On sait ce que l'on quitte, on ignore ce que l'on prend.

LES DEUX CHÈVRES.
Ne soyez entêté il est plus sage de céder le premier

LA COLOMBE ET LA FOURMI.
Il faut savoir s'entr'aider. On a souvent besoin d'un plus petit que soi.

LE RENARD ET LE CORBEAU
Méfiez-vous du flatteur, il vit toujours aux dépens de celui qui l'écoute.

SEASIDE TREASURES

Gathering seaside treasures involves creativity and experimentation! I'm constantly on the lookout for pieces that I can use in my ocean-inspired jewelry... old shells and pieces of mother-of-pearl, coral-colored nail head glass that I can glue onto charms, tiny mother-of-pearl buttons, and any sort of glass or brass fish charms. Try using a diamond bit with a Dremel drill to make small holes in natural materials such as shells and mother-of-pearl.

SOCIÉTÉ COOPÉRATIVE DE BOULANGERIE
EN COMMANDITE PAR ACTIONS
A CAPITAL VARIABLE

LA RENTRÉE SCOLAIRE

Aa Bb
Ccç Dd Ee
Ff Gg Hh Ii Jj Kk
Ll Mm Nn Oo Pp
Qq Rr Sſs Tt
UVu Ww Xx
Yy Zz

Summer's over, and it's time for la rentrée scolaire (back to school). Fun fact: while in the United States kids start in grade 1 and graduate in grade 12. the French system works in reverse. In elementary school, the grades aren't numbered. Then, at age 11, kids start grade 6, and then go on to 5th, 4th, 3rd, 2nd, 1st, and finally terminale.

Material Inspiration: brass flowers, antique type, old found bits and pieces that make up a mixed set of jewelry ideas.

USING RESINS

You can make your own charms by using your favorite artwork, bezels, and a resin solution. One of my favorites, Ice Resin, is self-doming and dries within 24 hours. To make charms, cut your artwork out to fit into each of your bezels, making sure to use bezels with at least a 1-mm cup. After mixing your resin solution completely, pour it into your bezel right up to the top and use a straw to gently blow out any air bubbles. Let the charms sit overnight to completely dry. If more of a bubble effect is desired, pour another layer of resin and allow it to cure for an additional 24 hours.

LA RENTRÉE SCOLAIRE NECKLACE

DIRECTIONS

Lightly glue the letters or images into the corresponding bezels. Following the directions on the resin package, pour slightly more resin into each bezel than you think you should, so it forms a bubble on top of the bezel. Let it dry for 24 hours.

Connect one end of each of the two chains to the watch clasp with a 5-mm jump ring. Connect a 5-mm jump ring to the other ends of the chains. Lay out letters/charms evenly in the center of the chain and attach them with jump rings going through both links of chain. Be sure to leave three or four links between each letter to attach a flower charm with a jump ring and a red bead with a head pin.

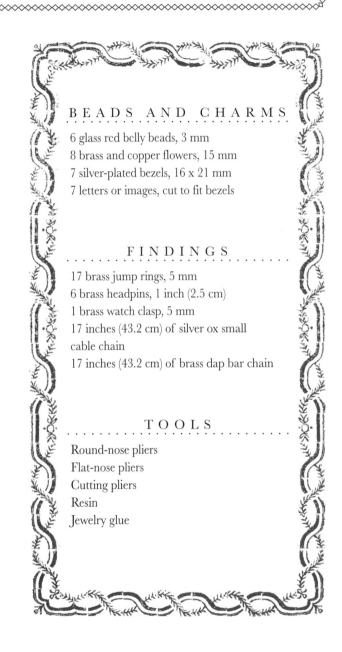

BEADS AND CHARMS

6 glass red belly beads, 3 mm
8 brass and copper flowers, 15 mm
7 silver-plated bezels, 16 x 21 mm
7 letters or images, cut to fit bezels

FINDINGS

17 brass jump rings, 5 mm
6 brass headpins, 1 inch (2.5 cm)
1 brass watch clasp, 5 mm
17 inches (43.2 cm) of silver ox small cable chain
17 inches (43.2 cm) of brass dap bar chain

TOOLS

Round-nose pliers
Flat-nose pliers
Cutting pliers
Resin
Jewelry glue

USING MIXED METALS
Often, it's hard to find all of the
right materials for your jewelry
designs in the same metal finish. I love
the look of mixed metals, including
antique brass, old silver, copper, and even
gold colors. Try using one color chain
and then blending in other colors. Set
your jewelry up on a board before you
connect each piece to give you a better
idea of the balance of metal colors.

LA RENTRÉE SCOLAIRE PIN

DIRECTIONS

Lightly glue the image onto the bezel. Following the directions on the package of resin, pour slightly more resin into the bezel than you think you should, so it forms a bubble on top of the bezel. Let the resin dry for 24 hours.

Glue the flower to the brass bar pin and let it dry. Using a jewelry hole punch, punch three 1-mm holes into the brass pin: One on either side and one at the bottom. Cut the chain into two pieces, one 2 ½ in. (6.4 cm) long and the other 3 ½ in. (8.9 cm) long. Using a 3-mm jump ring, attach the chain so it hangs slightly layered from the bar pin. Thread the eye pin with the red bead. Cut and link it closed onto the bottom of the eye pin. Attach the resin charm to the other end of the eye pin.

LA RENTRÉE SCOLAIRE EARRINGS

DIRECTIONS

Lightly glue the mother-of-pearl button into the bezel. Lightly glue the flower charm on top of the mother-of-pearl button. Mix and pour the resin until it forms a slight bubble on top of the bezel. Set aside to dry for at least 24 hours. When the resin is completely dry, thread one red bead onto the ear wire and glue it for security. Repeat to make the second earring.

BEADS

1 red fire-polished bead, 3 mm
1 metal flower, 17 mm
1 image, cut to fit bezel

FINDINGS

6 in. (15.2 cm) of tiny brass link chain
1 brass bezel, 17 x 18 mm
1 brass eye pin, 1 in. (2.5 cm)
2 brass jump rings, 3 mm
1 brass pin back, 1 in. (2.5 cm)
1 brass jewelry or scrapbooking decorative
    bar, 42 x 20 mm

TOOLS

Jewelry hole punch
Needle-nose pliers
Flat-nose pliers
Cutting pliers
Jewelry glue
Resin

BEADS

2 mother-of-pearl buttons, 17 mm
2 metal flowers, 10 mm
2 red fire-polished beads, 3 mm

FINDINGS

2 earring bezels, 17 mm

TOOLS

Resin
Jewelry glue

CHAIN

If you're not careful, collecting chain for jewelry designs can quickly become habit-forming! I look for all sorts of chain to work with—cable, figaro, open links, bar, and snake, just to name a few. I don't worry about the color of the chain, I like mixing the different colored chains in my work. If you find a raw chain that you would prefer in a darker color, simply dip raw chain into a small mixture of liver of sulphur and water, rinse and completely dry before using. This mixture also works well on sterling chain.

OCTOBRE

L'AUTOMNE

FROM THE START OF OCTOBER UNTIL EARLY NOVEMBER, CHESTNUTS ARE HARVESTED IN COLLOBRIERES, FRANCE. GATHERING THESE FRAGILE FRUITS, WHICH HAVE A SHORT LIFESPAN, WHEN FRESH, IS ALMOST ALWAYS A FAMILY AFFAIR. CHESTNUTS WERE ONCE A STAPLE OF LIFE IN HARD TIMES IN PARTS OF FRANCE. TODAY, THEY ARE A TREAT AND A FAVORITE FOR THE END-OF-YEAR HOLIDAYS, FIRE-ROASTED OR CANDIED, OR TRANSFORMED INTO CREAMY SAUCES OR SCRUMPTIOUS JAMS.

MATERIAL INSPIRATION: CARNELIANS, BROWNS, AND CORALS MAKE UP A SEASONAL PALETTE FOR THE AUTUMN-INSPIRED SET OF JEWELRY.

L'AUTOMNE NECKLACE

DIRECTIONS

Glue any and all cabochons to their bezels and set them aside to dry. On a large work surface, place the chain straight in front of you. Arrange your charms, beads, and buttons along the length of it, keeping in mind color, scale, and material. You want to attach a charm, bead, or button in every link.

Starting on the left side, connect one item to each link on the cable chain. When finished attaching all the pieces, connect the ends of the chain with the 8-mm jump ring.

BEADS, CHARMS, ETC.

This multijeweled necklace allows you to use up to at least 80 of the extra bits and pieces that make up your bead stash. The key here is working within one color palate. For my L'Automne Flower Necklace, I pulled out all my carnelian, rust, brown mother-of-pearl, and smoky-topaz colored glass beads and buttons. I accented these with brass-ox findings and chain, then added in a handful of burnished gold Lucite flowers. You'll find it helpful to have 3–4 mm crystal beads on hand to catch any wide-holed beads on head pins.

FINDINGS

34 in. (86.4 cm) of medium brass chain
Brass headpins, 1 inch (2.5 cm)—one for every bead
Brass jump rings, 3 mm and 8 mm—one for every charm and/or button
1 brass jump ring, 8 mm

TOOLS

Round-nose pliers
Flat-nose pliers
Cutting pliers
Jewelry glue

L'AUTOMNE BRACELET

DIRECTIONS

Cut the chain into 12 pieces, each 2 in. (5.1 cm) long.

Thread each crystal bead onto a ball-end head pin. Cut and loop them onto both small and large cable links in the chain. Thread an eye pin through each coral beaded bead and attach a chain link to either side. Continue this pattern for all 12 coral beads, to end up with a chain about 28 in. (71.1cm) long. Thread the elastic cord through each link in chain and then through the coral beads.

Continue this until you have one long strand of chain threaded onto the elastic cord. Carefully attach two ends of bracelet together by opening up an eye pin on the coral bead and attaching it to the chain. Gather both ends of the elastic cord together until bracelet fits around your wrist, and then knot off three times. (For this last part, you may need a friend to help measure your wrist size correctly.) Add a drop of glue to the knot and let it dry before wearing.

L'AUTOMN EARRINGS

DIRECTIONS

Cut the chain exactly in half. Attach each one to an earring post using a 3-mm jump ring. Set one earring post aside. Thread 26 coral beads onto head pins. Cut and loop each onto the chain, adding more beads to the top three-quarters of the chain and less to the bottom to create a cluster effect. For example, attach four coral beads in every link of chain until you reach the bottom three links. In the next link, reduce it to three beads, then two beads in the next-to-last link, and only one bead in the last link. Repeat to make the second earring.

BEADS

12 coral beaded beads, 11 mm
84 crystal beads, 4 mm

FINDINGS

84 brass ball-end head pins, 1 inch (2.5 cm)
24 in. (61 cm) of medium brass cable chain
24 in. (61 cm) of clear elastic cord (.7 mm)
12 brass eye pins, 1 inch (2.5 cm)

TOOLS

Round-nose pliers
Cutting pliers
Jewelry glue

BEADS

52 coral glass beads, 4 mm

FINDINGS

52 brass headpins, 1 in. (2.5 cm)
2 in. (5.1 cm) of brass chain
2 brass earring posts with backs
2 brass jump rings, 3 mm

TOOLS

Round-nose pliers
Cutting pliers

Favorite Finds

OLD CHARMS

Old charms come in all shapes, sizes, colors, and themes. Almost anything small can be made into a charm—dice, dominos, keys, tags, medals, rings, and even game pieces! Next time you're rooting through a box of old treasures, look for pieces that you can either glue onto a flat-back bezel or drill a hole through to hang with a jump ring. You'll be surprised how fast you gather up a drawer full of beautiful bits and bobs that will all look wonderful together on a necklace or bracelet.

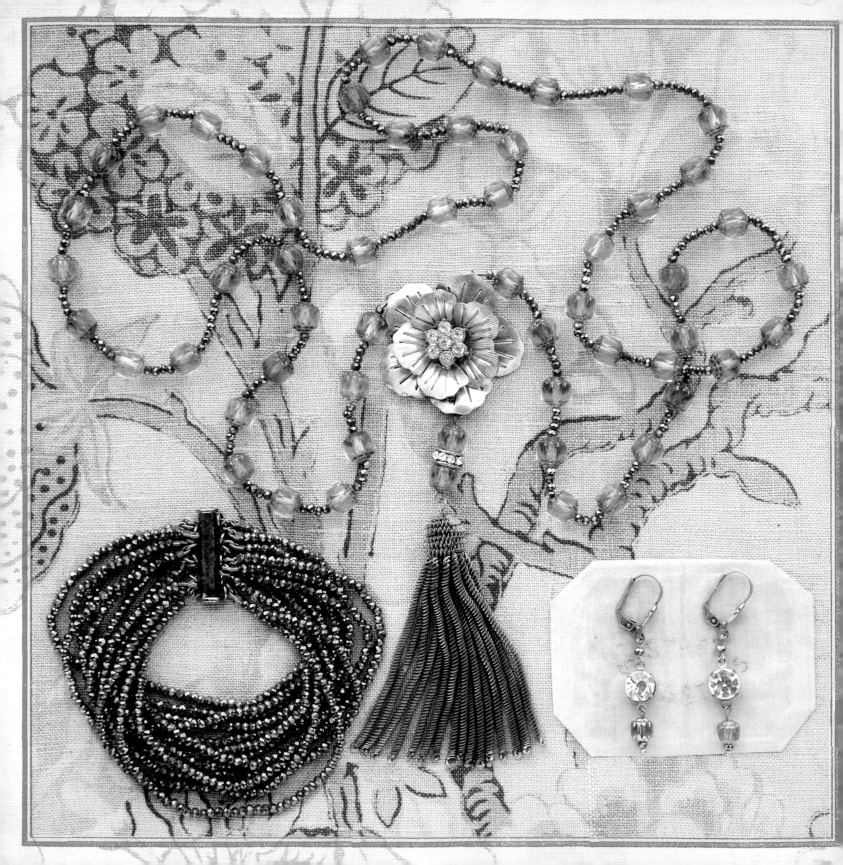

NOVEMBRE

LA TOUSSAINT

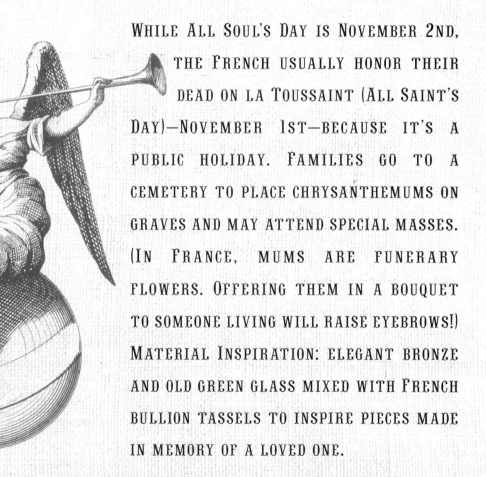

WHILE ALL SOUL'S DAY IS NOVEMBER 2ND, THE FRENCH USUALLY HONOR THEIR DEAD ON LA TOUSSAINT (ALL SAINT'S DAY)—NOVEMBER 1ST—BECAUSE IT'S A PUBLIC HOLIDAY. FAMILIES GO TO A CEMETERY TO PLACE CHRYSANTHEMUMS ON GRAVES AND MAY ATTEND SPECIAL MASSES. (IN FRANCE, MUMS ARE FUNERARY FLOWERS. OFFERING THEM IN A BOUQUET TO SOMEONE LIVING WILL RAISE EYEBROWS!) MATERIAL INSPIRATION: ELEGANT BRONZE AND OLD GREEN GLASS MIXED WITH FRENCH BULLION TASSELS TO INSPIRE PIECES MADE IN MEMORY OF A LOVED ONE.

MAKING A ROSARY-INSPIRED NECKLACE

Although this necklace looks like a
simple beaded necklace, the design
inspiration came from the silhouette of
an old rosary. I added in the flower and
tassel instead of the cross.

LA TOUSSAINT NECKLACE

DIRECTIONS

Knot the end of the silk bead cord (the fixed needle will be on the opposite end). String on one bronze crystal beads. Thread needle through ½ in. (1.3 cm) of French wire. Thread on a jump ring. Thread the needle through the first bead, and gently pull the thread while holding the jump ring in place with flat-nose pliers. This creates a small loop of French wire at the top of the first bead. Tie a knot after the first bead to hold it in place (you can also place a tiny drop of glue on the knot, if you like). Continue to thread through the next two beads, then cut the tail thread.

Thread on a green English cut bead, followed by 4 bronze crystal beads. Continue to thread on beads, following a rosary pattern (see the tip called Making a Rosary-Inspired Necklace) or the pattern of your choice, until you've strung 40 in. (1 m) of beads, or the desired length. When you've finished stringing, thread on another ½ in. (1.3 cm) of French wire and go back through the last bronze crystal bead to secure it. You can tie a knot, if possible, and add a tiny drop of glue on the knot, if you like. Trim off any excess thread.

Using jump rings, attach the ends of the strung beads to the flower charm. Thread a head pin through the tassel, then loop and close it. Thread an eye pin through a green bead, crystal rondelle, and another green bead, and link to the tassel. Using a jump ring, attach this tasseled component to the flower charm.

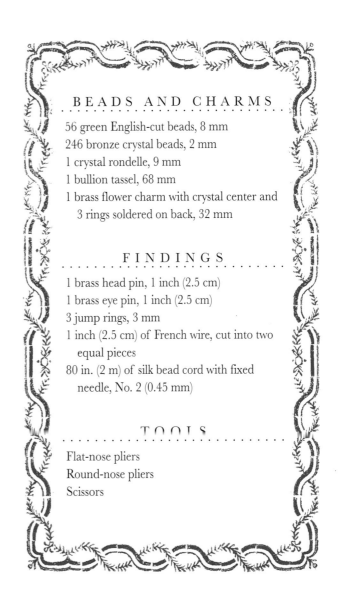

BEADS AND CHARMS

56 green English-cut beads, 8 mm
246 bronze crystal beads, 2 mm
1 crystal rondelle, 9 mm
1 bullion tassel, 68 mm
1 brass flower charm with crystal center and
   3 rings soldered on back, 32 mm

FINDINGS

1 brass head pin, 1 inch (2.5 cm)
1 brass eye pin, 1 inch (2.5 cm)
3 jump rings, 3 mm
1 inch (2.5 cm) of French wire, cut into two
   equal pieces
80 in. (2 m) of silk bead cord with fixed
   needle, No. 2 (0.45 mm)

TOOLS

Flat-nose pliers
Round-nose pliers
Scissors

USING FRENCH WIRE

I used to use a clam shell and crimp bead to close silk-strung necklaces or bracelets, but now I use a bit of French wire and a crimp bead so there's less stress on the silk cord. To use French wire, simply cut off a small piece 2 in. (about 5 cm) of the bullion wire, thread it onto your silk cord with needle attached, and to thread through your first two beads as well as a small jump ring. Using your needle, thread back through the beads and gently pull the thread while holding the jump ring in place with flat-nose pliers. Watching a French wire technique on You Tube is a great visual.

LA TOUSSAINT BRACELET

DIRECTIONS

Attach three strands to each of the four rings on either side of the clasp to make a 12-strand bracelet, as follows:

Knot the end of the silk bead cord (the needle will be on opposite end). String on three bronze crystal beads. Thread on ⅓ in. (10 mm) of French wire and a crimp bead. Thread on a jump ring. Thread the needle through the first bead, and gently pull the thread while holding the jump ring in place with flat-nose pliers. This creates a small loop of French wire at the top of the first bead. Using flat-nose pliers, squish the crimp bead closed. Thread on 85 bronze crystal beads. To finish the strand, thread on a crimp bead and then thread on ⅓ in. (10 mm) of French wire. Go back through the crimp bead with your needle and pinch it closed. Trim off any excess thread. Make two more strands just like this one. Using a 3-mm jump ring, gather the three strands and attach them to a soldered ring on one side of the clasp. Attach the loose ends of the strands on the other half of the clasp.

Continue making nine additional strands in the same manner. Attach them to the clasp in the same way.

LA TOUSSAINT EARRINGS

DIRECTIONS

Thread a bronze crystal bead and green English-cut bead onto a ball end head pin. Cut and loop the head pin closed; as you do this, attach it to one connecting ring on the bezel holding the crystal. Thread an eye pin through a bronze crystal bead. Cut and loop it closed through the other connecting ring of the bezel. Attach the loop in the eye pin onto the ear wire. Repeat to make the second earring.

BEADS

1,056 bronze crystal beads, 2 mm
  (88/each strand)

FINDINGS

24 crimp beads, 2 mm
5 in. (12.7 cm) of French wire
24 brass crimp beads
24 jump rings, 3 mm
1 brass 4-ring slide clasp
80 in. (2 m) of silk bead cord with fixed
  needle, No. 2 (0.45 mm)

TOOLS

Flat-nose pliers
Scissors

BEADS

2 green English-cut beads, 6 mm
4 bronze crystal beads, 2 mm
2 rhinestones in cup bezel with two
  connecting rings, 8 mm

FINDINGS

2 brass ball end head pins, 1 inch (2.5 cm)
2 brass eye pins, 1 inch (2.5 cm)
2 brass French lever-back ear wires

TOOLS

Round-nose pliers
Cutting pliers

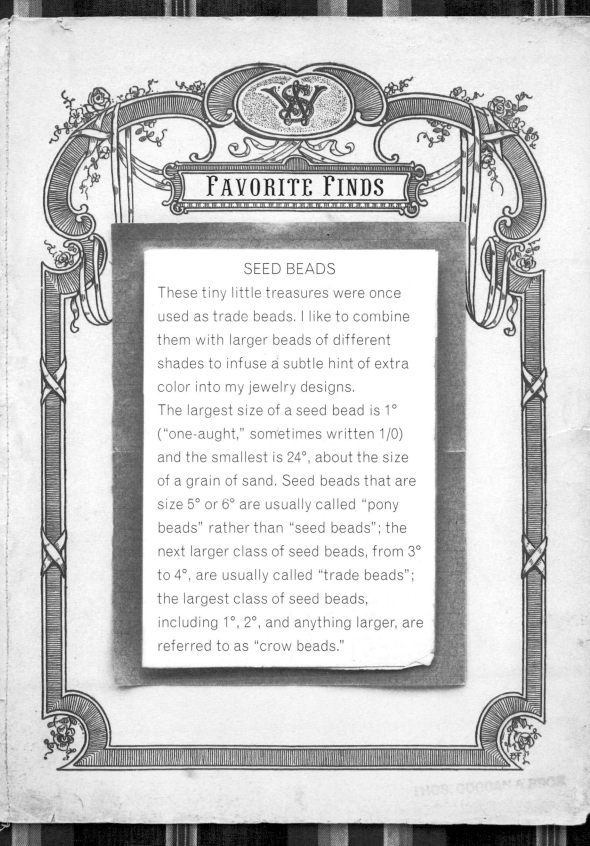

SEED BEADS

These tiny little treasures were once used as trade beads. I like to combine them with larger beads of different shades to infuse a subtle hint of extra color into my jewelry designs.

The largest size of a seed bead is 1° ("one-aught," sometimes written 1/0) and the smallest is 24°, about the size of a grain of sand. Seed beads that are size 5° or 6° are usually called "pony beads" rather than "seed beads"; the next larger class of seed beads, from 3° to 4°, are usually called "trade beads"; the largest class of seed beads, including 1°, 2°, and anything larger, are referred to as "crow beads."

DÉCEMBRE

LE RÉVEILLON

Back in the days when most French people attended midnight mass to celebrate Christmas, le Réveillon was the big feast that followed. While different regions of France have their own traditional menus, every Réveillon in the nation is certain to end with a bûche de Nöel, a layered sponge cake shaped to look like a log, with frosting applied to resemble bark and powdered sugar as snow. The cake derives from pagan solstice celebrations involving Yule logs.

Material Inspiration: mother-of-pearl buttons, red glass beads, and handmade tassels for a bit of dazzle for the holidays.

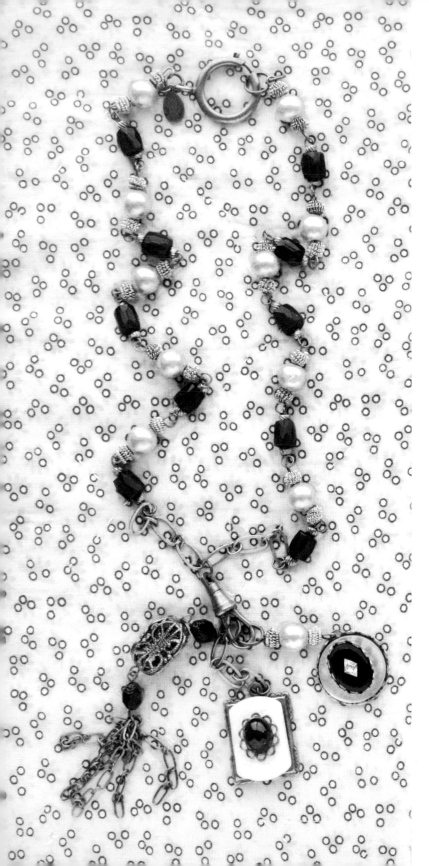

LE RÉVEILLON NECKLACE

DIRECTIONS

Glue the mother-of-pearl cabochons onto the corresponding bezels and set aside to dry. Glue the 15 x 11-mm and the 8 x 10-mm cabochon onto their respective bezels and allow to dry. Glue the 15 x 11-mm cabochon and its bezel onto the round mother-of-pearl charm. Glue the 8 x 10-mm cabochon and its bezel onto the rectangular mother-of-pearl charm. Set aside to dry. Cut the medium-size chain into three equal pieces. Cut the small cable chain into seven equal pieces. Set aside. In this section, you'll make the back of the necklace. Thread 10 eye pins with the following (which we'll call Pattern 1): one coiled wire bead, one glass pearl, and one coiled wire bead. Then thread 10 of the eye pins with the following (which is Pattern 2): one torse or textured brass bead, one faceted glass tube bead, and one torse or textured brass bead. Cut the wire down a bit on all 20 eye pins. Then make loops, linking five Pattern 1 and five Pattern 2 eye pins—alternate them—to make a rosary chain. Repeat to make an identical rosary chain. At one end of one rosary chain, attach a 5-mm jump ring, and then attach an 8-mm jump ring to that. On the corresponding end of the other rosary chain, attach a 5-mm jump ring and the 12-mm clasp.

For the front of your necklace, use a 3-mm jump ring to attach one piece of the medium cable chain to one free end of a rosary chain. Repeat to attach another piece of chain to the free end of the other rosary chain. Connect the two pieces of chain using a 5-mm jump ring, but before closing it, slip in the 20-mm swivel clasp, which will act as the charm holder.

Bend back one of the scallops on the round mother-of-pearl bezel. To make the first charm, thread a coiled wire bead, a glass pearl, and another coiled wire bead onto a head pin, and loop it onto the bent-back scallop on the round bezel.

To make the second charm, thread an eye pin through a 5 x 7-mm faceted bead, cut the wire, and loop it closed. Thread an eye pin through the filigree bead, cut the wire, and loop it closed while hooking into a loop on the faceted bead. Thread an eye pin onto the remaining 5 x 7-mm faceted bead, cut the wire, and loop it onto the filigree bead. Catch the seven pieces of small cable chain onto a 3-mm jump ring and then connect it to the loop in the previously made eye pin with a faceted bead on it.

For the third charm, connect the remaining piece of medium cable chain to the rectangular mother-of-pearl charm using a 3-mm jump ring. Attach an 8-mm jump ring to each of the charms, so that they can be connected to the swivel clasp easily. Using the large jump rings allows you to put on or take off the charms, depending upon how many you want to wear at a time.

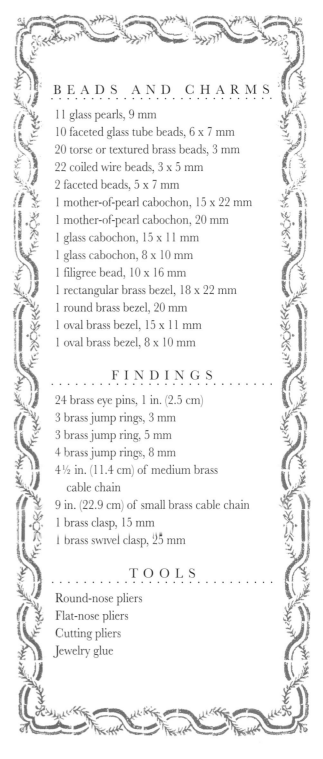

BEADS AND CHARMS

11 glass pearls, 9 mm
10 faceted glass tube beads, 6 x 7 mm
20 torse or textured brass beads, 3 mm
22 coiled wire beads, 3 x 5 mm
2 faceted beads, 5 x 7 mm
1 mother-of-pearl cabochon, 15 x 22 mm
1 mother-of-pearl cabochon, 20 mm
1 glass cabochon, 15 x 11 mm
1 glass cabochon, 8 x 10 mm
1 filigree bead, 10 x 16 mm
1 rectangular brass bezel, 18 x 22 mm
1 round brass bezel, 20 mm
1 oval brass bezel, 15 x 11 mm
1 oval brass bezel, 8 x 10 mm

FINDINGS

24 brass eye pins, 1 in. (2.5 cm)
3 brass jump rings, 3 mm
3 brass jump ring, 5 mm
4 brass jump rings, 8 mm
4½ in. (11.4 cm) of medium brass cable chain
9 in. (22.9 cm) of small brass cable chain
1 brass clasp, 15 mm
1 brass swivel clasp, 25 mm

TOOLS

Round-nose pliers
Flat-nose pliers
Cutting pliers
Jewelry glue

MAKING TASSELS

Tassels are a fun way to add a bit of glamour to any of your jewelry. Make them out of chain, beads, or fiber, or look for old tassels on clothing, belts, or pillows to snip off and add to your designs. Try using a bead cap as the top of a tassel and then add beads using eye pins—you can make them any length you like or add graduating beads to mix it up a bit.

LA RÉVEILLON BRACELET

DIRECTIONS

Imagine the bezels are clocks. On each one, bend back a scallop at the 12 and the 6. Glue a mother-of-pearl cabochon into each bezel and set them aside to dry. Link the bezels together using a 5-mm jump ring between each (slide the jump rings into the bent-back scallops); make sure they all face the same direction. At one end, attach the clasp, using a 5-mm jump ring. At the other end, attach an 8-mm jump ring, and attach the other 8-mm jump ring into it. Thread one faceted bead onto each head pin, cut the wire, and loop one onto either side of each of the 5-mm jump rings.

LA RÉVEILLON EARRINGS

DIRECTIONS

Thread an eye pin through a faceted bead, cut the wire, and loop it onto the ear wire. Thread an eye pin through a filigree bead, cut the wire, and loop it onto the free end of the faceted bead. Thread an eye pin through another faceted bead, cut, and loop it onto the free end of the filigree bead. Set aside, and repeat to start the second earring. Cut the chain into 14 equal pieces.

Collect seven pieces of chain onto a jump ring and then connect it to the free loop on the eye pin with a faceted bead on it. Repeat to finish the second earring.

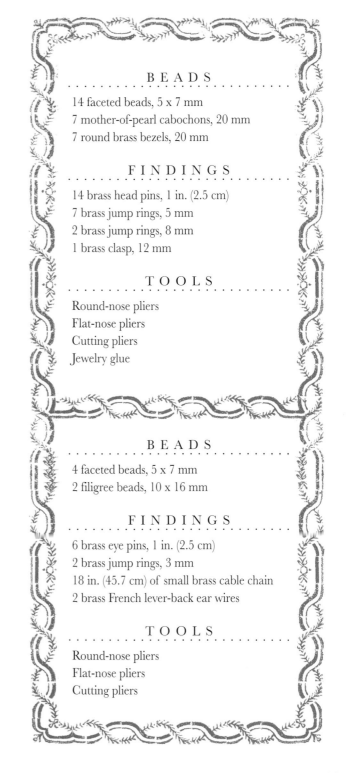

BEADS

14 faceted beads, 5 x 7 mm
7 mother-of-pearl cabochons, 20 mm
7 round brass bezels, 20 mm

FINDINGS

14 brass head pins, 1 in. (2.5 cm)
7 brass jump rings, 5 mm
2 brass jump rings, 8 mm
1 brass clasp, 12 mm

TOOLS

Round-nose pliers
Flat-nose pliers
Cutting pliers
Jewelry glue

BEADS

4 faceted beads, 5 x 7 mm
2 filigree beads, 10 x 16 mm

FINDINGS

6 brass eye pins, 1 in. (2.5 cm)
2 brass jump rings, 3 mm
18 in. (45.7 cm) of small brass cable chain
2 brass French lever-back ear wires

TOOLS

Round-nose pliers
Flat-nose pliers
Cutting pliers

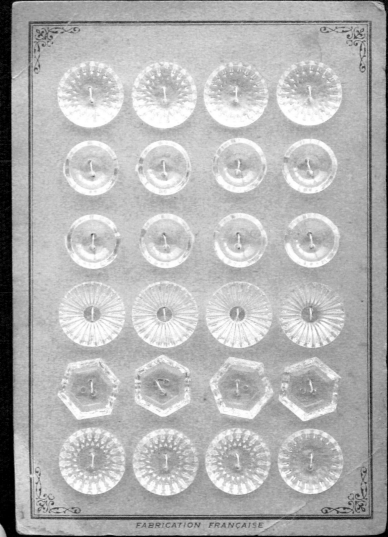

FABRICATION FRANÇAISE

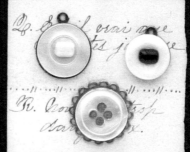

Favorite Finds

OLD BUTTONS

I look for bags of old mother-of-pearl buttons with metal flat-back shanks that will snip off easily to leave a flat-back mother-of-pearl cabochon. These buttons usually fit perfectly into bezels to make charms. If the buttons don't have shanks that can be cut off, you can still use them in your jewelry—just thread them through a head pin, cut it, and loop it onto a chain.

We hadn't crafted a book in quite a few years and along the way…
I must have forgotten how many people and how much work goes
into a book project! The idea to do another jewelry book was
Nathalie Monru's idea (our editor at Lark) She loved the idea of us
designing a year of jewelry inspired by the French Holidays…as both
of her parents were born in France. We enlisted Nathalie's French
mom, Jeanine Monru, to help us with our chapter openers…thanks
Nathalie and Jeanine for all of your guidance and knowledge! At
the eleventh hour, when I could no longer bead another bead, Beth
Reames came to my rescue and pulled our collections together…
thank you Beth for your skill, taste, and talent. Also at the eleventh
hour, John Foster came along and took the reins and guided us
through the final stages of our project…thanks John for stepping
in and never missing a beat! Thank you always Molly for your keen
typing and editing skills. Jon Zabala and I could not do another book
without the support of our daughter Sofia…who is the final word on
all of our designs and ideas. She has grown into an artist by simply
absorbing our lifestyle and we cannot wait to see where she goes
from here! And finally, thank you to everyone who has purchased
my jewelry, made our jewelry kits, and supported the idea of French
General craft over the many years!

Kaari

ABOUT THE AUTHOR

Kaari Meng began designing jewelry for Bergdorf Goodman after graduating from the jewelry program at FIT in New York City. In need of a hat pin, Kaari designed a collection of pins and presented them to the jewelry buyer at the monthly open-buy day. The buyer at Bergdorf's bought all of Kaari's designs and requested a full collection of jewelry for their cases. Using vintage glass beads, buttons, and notions, Kaari created a unique look that appealed to many women looking for something different. Kaari began designing for Anthropology when they opened their first store in Philadelphia in 1992. For many years, Anthropologie and Kaari enjoyed working and designing together—all of the jewelry pieces Kaari designed used her vast collection of antique beads found all over the world.

In 1997, the year Kaari's daughter Sofia was born, the business evolved into another company, French General, which originally began as a retail store on Crosby Street in New York's Soho district. Filled with apothecary jars brimming with vintage notions, Kaari and her sister Molly began selling a French-inspired lifestyle that included textiles, notions, ephemera, and household items only found in France. In 2003, Kaari and her family moved to Los Angeles and set up French General in an old Spanish-style warehouse, on the edge of town and opened up one day a week for people to come in and browse their ever changing collections that they brought on yearly trips to the South of France.

Offering a variety of vintage craft workshops and kits, Kaari, and her husband, JZ, eventually wrote five books highlighting all of the elements the French General brand had evolved into:

French-Inspired Home (Lark/Sterling),

French-Inspired Jewelry (Lark/Sterling),

Home Sewn (Chronicle),

Handmade Soirées (Chronicle), and

*Treasured Notions (*Chronicle)

were all written and designed by French General.

French General also designs quilting fabric for Moda; scrapbooking materials, including paper, notion, and dies for Sizzix; as well as a line of home decorating fabric, trim, and wallpaper for Fabricut.

And to relax...Kaari and her posse take groups of women to the South of France every summer to live in an eighteenth-century chateau. For four weeks, four different groups of creative women come and learn to live like rural French women—visiting the flea markets, local villages, and artisans. Kaari draws on her summers in France as her inspiration to continue to create the French General lifestyle.

INDEX